12 Secret Sales Hacks
That Have Stood The Test Of Time

Discover these powerful strategies all top entrepreneurs are using now to build their empires.

Laura Burton

Copyright © 2019 by Laura Burton

All rights reserved. No part of this publication may be reproduced, distributed or transmitted in any form or by any means, without prior written permission.

Laura Burton
416 Sales
www.416sales.com

12 Secret Sales Hacks That Have Stood The Test Of Time / Laura Burton. – 1st edition.

For my dad, who taught me the most about sales. For my husband, who is my rock. For my family who love me and who I love. For my friends and colleagues who have been amazing people in my life. Thank you all!

For all of you who are reading this book....
Sell Well and Sell Often.

CONTENTS

Why Sales? 7
Where These 12 Secrets Came From 13
Secret 1 Persevere - PT Barnum 17
Secret 2 Whatever You Do, Do It With All Your Might - PT Barnum 21
Secret 3 Don't Get Above Your Business - PT Barnum 27
Secret 4 Be Systematic - PT Barnum 33
Secret 5 Advertise Your Business - PT Barnum 37
Secret 6 Be Polite And Kind To Your Customers - PT Barnum 41
Secret 7 The Mind Of The Salesman – William Walker Atkinson ... 45
Secret 8 The Mind Of The Buyer - William Walker Atkinson 57
Secret 9 The Psychology Of Purchase - William Walker Atkinson .. 61
Secret 10 The Approach - William Walker Atkinson 77
Secret 11 The Demonstration - William Walker Atkinson 93
Secret 12 The Closing - William Walker Atkinson 111
Conclusion 125

CHAPTER ONE

Why Sales?

My name is Laura Burton. I'm The Secret Sales Hacks Expert. I'm a sales professional, sales coach. I've been selling most of my life. When I was a little girl, probably 8 yrs old, I went up to my dad on the couch in our family room. He was working on something. And I asked him if I could go somewhere. I don't remember what I asked. I was 8. I'm 56 now. He wasn't in the mood to be interrupted and he told me. NO.

My dad was my hero. I loved my dad so much. And his approval meant the world to me. And when he said, "No", in that tone of voice, I knew he meant it. Needless to say. I was upset. But I didn't argue with him. I stood there for a minute and my eyes teared up and I wanted to say something but I didn't know what to say. So I started walking away.

He looked up from his work and noticed that I was visibly upset when I turned to leave the room. Well the guilt must have killed him. He was a salesman after all. He had his own advertising agency. So he called me back. And by this time I was ready to cry. So I walked back over to him and he asked me, "Laura. Do you really want to do this?"

And I was sniffling a bit. And he asked again. Do you really want to go? And with my quivering lips, teary eyes, and crackling voice I looked back at him and said, "Yes". He probably wanted to crawl under the couch at that point. It was right then and there that he gave me my first lesson in sales. And I've been a closer ever since.

I've been in sales over 30 years now. I've sold B2C, B2B, face-to-face, insides phone sales, I've done cold calls, warm leads, inbound leads, opening, closing, and have been a top closer for over 25 years. At one point, I sold advertising for the Jewish Israeli Yellow Pages in Los Angeles. A friend of mine heard I was doing that and recruited me for her sales team.

She basically told me, "If you can sell that, you can sell anything." So I worked in the dating industry for awhile as an opener. We were called Dating Consultants so people would want to talk to us. And when the economy was good openers were making up to $80k/year. I got there after the economy crash so I missed the peak of that. But I learned a lot doing it.

I never really intended to be a sales person. I mean, why do that? It wasn't honored like being a doctor or lawyer. I was an artist when I was younger. I loved painting, drawing, and playing music. I was more motivated to follow my heart than to follow a dollar. I was a free spirit and worked different jobs to pay bills to support my art pursuits. I could always find jobs.

Whenever I needed work, I would pull out the business white pages and start at the letter A or Z. This was before the internet. Then I would call companies with cool sounding names. A lot of people were confused with my call and would ask me why I was calling them. I'd tell them I needed a job and their company sounded like it would be a great place to work.

By the time I was half way through the alphabet, ~200 calls later, I would land 8 - 10 interviews and get hired for a sales job. I was having fun, I loved people, I loved the products I was selling and I loved hooking people up with something they were going to LOVE. I loved selling because it didn't seem like selling. I was an artist helping people out to make extra money.

When I was 36 years old, I was exposed to chemicals at a store I was working at and wound up with a chemical injury. The fancy name is environmental illness. It was the most difficult, confusing, scary experience I ever had in my life. At one point, I wasn't able to walk a mile. And the doctors weren't very helpful. They told me I would just get worse. But that wasn't my truth.

What should have been the prime time of my career growth turned into 5 yrs of disability being sick everyday barely functioning. Everyone I knew was killing it. I was on my couch. It was an immune disorder that came with a lot of issues. Basically, I needed to stay away from chemicals, dust, fumes, and stress. I looked at my doctor when he told me that and I asked him, "How?"

I lived in LA. The land of cars and I was supposed to stay away from car exhaust among other things. I lived in San Fernando Valley with over 800,000 other people who all had cars and drove them everyday. There are tens of thousands of unregulated chemicals on the market, and roughly **2,000** new chemicals introduced each year. That's not counting the regulated ones.

It was a journey I really wouldn't have chosen for myself. I mean, who wants to be sick all the time? Not, me. But it did prepare me for when my husband was diagnosed with multiple sclerosis 6 years into our marriage when I was older. And coming through a long process that wasn't easy also gave me a foundation that had unexpected benefits. Determined persistence.

After lots of changes, lots of crying, lots of learning, lots of struggles, lots of disappointment, lots of sadness, lots of perspective adjustments, and lots of asking, "What can I do now?", I became a different person. I was removed from regular life. If I was exposed to chemicals when I was out, I was down for 2 days. I had extreme fatigue a lot. My life basically sucked.

Little by little I came across things that helped me get better. After 3 yrs of adopting new lifestyle habits, I was able to function like a normal person again. I hadn't worked in 6 years. I worked for realtors for awhile right when the housing crash was about to hit. Then other jobs. After my dating industry gig, my husband suggested that I get a writing job since I like writing so much.

I took a $12/hour job as a project manager for an internet marketing company. The company posted their job on Craigslist as a "writing" job. I guess they thought if you were a writer you could be articulate when you spoke with clients and you could write a decent email. They wanted proper sentences, not the texting lingo that so many young adults are accustomed to.

When I figured out what I could sell to clients to make extra money, I became one of the top sales people in the company. The Sales Director wanted me to transfer to the sales department and work for him, but I wasn't really interested. Later, I was promoted to oversee a new sales office as a closer manager. When you can close deals no one wants you off the phone.

I worked in internet marketing sales for over 7 years. Internet marketing is extremely competitive. Some business owners are called 30 - 40 times a week by telemarketers selling something that's going to be amazing for their marketing. That's not including the 50-100 emails that land in their inbox and spam. It's exhausting for business owners at times.

I've had varying roles, sold a lot of marketing services, managed closers, and trained hundreds of sales reps. I also personally did website analyses for over 15,000 business owners, managers, and IT people. And what I've learned is that sales is the most important thing that a lot of people don't ever learn how to do well if at all. And they are missing out.

The truth is, selling is fun when you're selling a great product that people need and value. There's just so much to do, and so many options, and so much information, and everyone has a secret. I have 12 Secrets here in this book. Where is a person supposed to start? And that is a great question. That is the million dollar question people ask themselves everyday.

So I decided to take a giant leap of faith to create something to give you everything you need to be more successful at sales. This book is your first step. This book is designed to give you time tested strategies, ways of approaching sales that have been used for more than a century. They are so good that all top entrepreneurs today are using them. And in this book they are yours.

My goal for this book, and other offers you'll get from me, was to create a way to give YOU, the reader, everything you need to be successful at sales. I've said it twice because it's important. This was created to give you the exact knowledge and tools you need to get better at sales for your business. It's the one thing that everyone should learn to be happier in their life.

I've consistently become the top closer in every company I've ever sold for. I want you to be the top closer for yourself. When you think of sales, I want you to have a great feeling in your heart, a big smile on your face, and so much confidence that you can really shine as the best person you really are. Sales is about selling YOU. You helping other people get what they want.

And this is how you're going to do it. In this book, I'm going to share sales knowledge and wisdom and experience that has been handed down through the generations from the beginning of the industrial revolution to the technology evolution of sales and marketing where we are today. When you learn this I want you to start seeing patterns in your life.

I want you to recognize how this information has been used in different forms. I want you to see how effective these strategies have sold you products and services before and how effective they will be for you when you start to implement them for your own business. And send me an email if you have any questions at laura@416sales.com

CHAPTER TWO

Where These 12 Secrets Came From

When I was close to the end of my time on disability, I met a girl named Lorrie Morgan that was making 6 figures selling copywriting courses on the internet. That intrigued me. She got her start in 1999 and was doing amazing things. Since I had a lot of time, I started looking at what she and her compadres were doing and it was fascinating. The technology was mind blowing.

This was around 2005, before mainstream businesses had caught on that this internet thing was a viable market place. I'm not much of a tech person and I wasn't back to normal so I just took in what I saw going on. In 2011, when I got into internet marketing, it was amazing to see how the technology evolved. Having grown up with advertising in my house I noticed something.

The screens had changed but the basic building blocks of sales were pretty much the same. The only real difference now is the speed at which we can create and distribute information. And as I've been researching sales, (I love learning new things), I noticed that a lot of the secrets being taught were pretty similar as well. I got the idea for this book when I was taking a class.

The guy teaching it mentioned PT Barnum being great at sales and the movie The Greatest Showman. I was curious about it so I looked him up. Then I found a sales book he wrote called, The Art of Getting

Money. He lived from 1810 - 1891. That made me curious about other sales books from around the same time period. Then I found another sales book by William Walker Atkinson, called The Psychology of Salesmanship. He lived from 1862 - 1932.

Then I thought, "All this sales gold has been handed down from previous generations". I know I learned from my dad and my experience selling. There are sales giants sharing information and sales organizations generating a lot of content. Tons of classes are available online and offline. It's really valuable stuff. There are a lot of people making a lot of money selling sales.

What I also noticed is that even with all this knowledge and all these great catch phrases, a lot of entrepreneurs and salespeople are still struggling with sales. Knowing what to do is not the same as being able to actually do it. Everyone has their talent. Everyone has their thing. Not everyone can implement what they've learned without a process to follow.

I've done a lot of sales training that focuses on the mechanics of how things are done on sales calls, follow up, attitude, following a system, and being your amazing wonderful self. Some reps I trained told me they never had any training like that before and they had worked at Fortune 500 companies. I was surprised to hear that. It made me wonder about what I was doing.

As more opportunities came up for me to talk to people about sales, I realized that for many people, something is missing when they venture into the world of dreams of what can be and how they should get there. In some cases, people need a bridge. They need things they can easily implement to get results. They need to understand the process more.

I've helped sales people become top closers many times. I realized that for me it was time to do that at a different level on a different platform in a different way. It also occurred to me that people need foundational knowledge presented with perspective: Perspective of where they are now with perspective of how to do things day in and day out, over and over and over again.

I decided to use those sources of information that are readily available to share. I wanted to put together what I believe are the most important 12 "Secrets" you can use right now to improve your sales, business, and personal performance. I believe sales is something everyone can and should learn. I was always able to earn a living because I could sell.

A lot of entrepreneurs and small business owners are struggling with sales for their businesses. It's a new world when bringing in revenue is on you to close deals, get on the phone, service a customer, or send another email out. What seems like a good idea doesn't always work. We know what we like. We aren't our customers. Without sales there isn't a business.

I chose the books by Phineas Taylor (PT) Barnum and William Walker Atkinsonto pull these 12 Secrets from based on how often I have come across these secrets, how I have used them, and how relevant they are. PT Barnum is probably more known of the two, particularly from the recent movie, The Greatest Showman. Here is why I choose them.

The Art of Getting Money by PT Barnum. His overall approach is to keep things in perspective, stay focused, and work really hard. He was a master at understanding how to captivate audiences with something unusual and out of the ordinary. At times, he fabricated truth to make money, but his approach to business and his drive for success are being used here.

The Psychology of Salesmanship by William Walker Atkinson. What got my attention here is that he only wrote one book about sales. Everything else he wrote was about new thought, the occult, mind reading, yoga, and everything we would consider new age today. His discussion of sales is based on face to face sales. His quotes and insights get to the heart of a sales person.

I want you to be able to read what they have said about things and share some stories with you. I want you to be able to see for yourself how these ideas are woven into the fabric of our culture so you can be aware of what you are being sold and how to sell better for yourself. If you've studied any of the current sales greats, you'll recognize their material from here.

CHAPTER THREE

Secret 1
Persevere - PT Barnum

When a man is in the right path, he must persevere. I speak of this because there are some persons who are "born tired;" naturally lazy and possessing no self-reliance and no perseverance. But they can cultivate these qualities, as Davy Crockett said:

"This thing remember, when I am dead: Be sure you are right, then go ahead."

It is this go-aheaditiveness, this determination not to let the "horrors" or the "blues" take possession of you, so as to make you relax your energies in the struggle for independence, which you must cultivate.

How many have almost reached the goal of their ambition, but, losing faith in themselves, have relaxed their energies, and the golden prize has been lost forever.

It is, no doubt, often true, as Shakespeare says:

"There is a tide in the affairs of men, Which, taken at the flood, leads on to fortune."

If you hesitate, some bolder hand will stretch out before you and get the prize. Remember the proverb of Solomon: "He becometh poor that dealeth with a slack hand; but the hand of the diligent maketh rich."

Perseverance is sometimes but another word for self-reliance. Many persons naturally look on the dark side of life, and borrow trouble. They are born so. Then they ask for advice, and they will be governed by one wind and blown by another, and cannot rely upon themselves. Until you can get so that you can rely upon yourself, you need not expect to succeed.

I have known men, personally, who have met with pecuniary reverses, and absolutely committed suicide, because they thought they could never overcome their misfortune. But I have known others who have met more serious financial difficulties, and have bridged them over by simple perseverance, aided by a firm belief that they were doing justly, and that Providence would "overcome evil with good." You will see this illustrated in any sphere of life.

Take two generals; both understand military tactics, both educated at West Point, if you please, both equally gifted; yet one, having this principle of perseverance, and the other lacking it, the former will succeed in his profession, while the latter will fail. One may hear the cry, "the enemy are coming, and they have got cannon."

"Got cannon?" says the hesitating general.

"Yes."

"Then halt every man."

He wants time to reflect; his hesitation is his ruin; the enemy passes unmolested, or overwhelms him; while on the other hand, the general of pluck, perseverance and self-reliance, goes into battle with a will, and, amid the clash of arms, the booming of cannon, the shrieks of the wounded, and the moans of the dying, you will see this man persevering, going on, cutting and slashing his way through with unwavering determination, inspiring his soldiers to deeds of fortitude, valor, and triumph.

A lot of people tend to give up. When I was younger and was impatient, my dad used to tell me not to have a television mentality. What he meant by that was things take longer than you might think. TV shows are a ½ hour, an hour. Most films are 1 ½ hours - 3 hours. Time is distorted in stories that are condensed for entertainment. You usually only fail if you quit.

I didn't readily give up being impatient until my dad talked to me about timing. Perfect timing is worth waiting for. Waiting for the sake of waiting didn't work for me. And the underlying theme of perseverance has to do with the person's mental attitude. You have to have it in your mind to persevere. You have to decide you're going to finish something even if it gets hard.

Successful entrepreneurs all have stories of when things got bad, when things didn't work out. My dad used to tell me, "If you fall into a puddle of water and you're covered in mud, get up, get yourself washed up, put on clean clothes and move on. Don't sit in the puddle complaining waiting for someone to come along to save you. Get up and get yourself cleaned up."

Perseverance in sales has to do with staying focused on selling. If you need to make calls, make calls. If you need to send out emails, send emails. If you need to run ads, run ads. If it's customer service, do that. Keep doing what is needed everyday, day after day. Realize the progress you're making and keep your momentum going by sticking with it.

CHAPTER FOUR

Secret 2
Whatever You Do, Do It With All Your Might - PT Barnum

Work at it, if necessary, early and late, in season and out of season, not leaving a stone unturned, and never deferring for a single hour that which can be done just as well now. The old proverb is full of truth and meaning, "Whatever is worth doing at all, is worth doing well." Many a man acquires a fortune by doing his business thoroughly, while his neighbor remains poor for life, because he only half does it. Ambition, energy, industry, perseverance, are indispensable requisites for success in business.

Fortune always favors the brave, and never helps a man who does not help himself. It won't do to spend your time like Mr. Micawber, in waiting for something to "turn up." To such men one of two things usually "turns up:" the poorhouse or the jail; for idleness breeds bad habits, and clothes a man in rags. The poor spendthrift vagabond says to a rich man:

"I have discovered there is enough money in the world for all of us, if it was equally divided; this must be done, and we shall all be happy together."

"But," was the response, "if everybody was like you, it would be spent in two months, and what would you do then?"

"Oh! divide again; keep dividing, of course!"

I was recently reading in a London paper an account of a like philosophic pauper who was kicked out of a cheap boarding-house because he could not pay his bill, but he had a roll of papers sticking out of his coat pocket, which, upon examination, proved to be his plan for paying off the national debt of England without the aid of a penny. People have got to do as Cromwell said: "not only trust in Providence, but keep the powder dry." Do your part of the work, or you cannot succeed. Mahomet, one night, while encamping in the desert, overheard one of his fatigued followers remark: "I will loose my camel, and trust it to God!" "No, no, not so," said the prophet, "tie thy camel, and trust it to God!" Do all you can for yourselves, and then trust to Providence, or luck, or whatever you please to call it, for the rest.

DEPEND UPON YOUR OWN PERSONAL EXERTIONS.

The eye of the employer is often worth more than the hands of a dozen employees. In the nature of things, an agent cannot be so faithful to his employer as to himself. Many who are employers will call to mind instances where the best employees have overlooked important points which could not have escaped their own observation as a proprietor. No man has a right to expect to succeed in life unless he understands his business, and nobody can understand his business thoroughly unless he learns it by personal application and experience. A man may be a manufacturer: he has got to learn the many details of his business personally; he will learn something every day, and he will find he will make mistakes nearly every day. And these very mistakes are helps to him in the way of experiences if he but heeds them. He will be like the Yankee tin-peddler, who, having been cheated as to quality in the purchase of his merchandise, said: "All right, there's a little information to be gained every day; I will never be cheated in that way again." Thus a man buys his experience, and it is the best kind if not purchased at too dear a rate.

I hold that every man should, like Cuvier, the French naturalist, thoroughly know his business. So proficient was he in the study of natural history, that you might bring to him the bone, or even a section of a bone of an animal which he had never seen described, and, reasoning from analogy, he would be able to draw a picture of the object from which the bone had been taken. On one occasion his students attempted to deceive him. They rolled one of their number in a cow skin and put him under the professor's table as a new specimen. When the philosopher came into the room, some of the students asked him what animal it was. Suddenly the animal said "I am the devil and I am going to eat you." It was but natural that Cuvier should desire to classify this creature, and examining it intently, he said:

"Divided hoof; graminivorous! It cannot be done."

He knew that an animal with a split hoof must live upon grass and grain, or other kind of vegetation, and would not be inclined to eat flesh, dead or alive, so he considered himself perfectly safe. The possession of a perfect knowledge of your business is an absolute necessity in order to insure success.

Among the maxims of the elder Rothschild was one, all apparent paradox: "Be cautious and bold." This seems to be a contradiction in terms, but it is not, and there is great wisdom in the maxim. It is, in fact, a condensed statement of what I have already said. It is to say; "you must exercise your caution in laying your plans, but be bold in carrying them out." A man who is all caution, will never dare to take hold and be successful; and a man who is all boldness, is merely reckless, and must eventually fail. A man may go on "'change" and make fifty, or one hundred thousand dollars in speculating in stocks, at a single operation. But if he has simple boldness without caution, it is mere chance, and what he gains to-day he will lose to-morrow. You must have both the caution and the boldness, to insure success.

The Rothschilds have another maxim: "Never have anything to do with an unlucky man or place." That is to say, never have anything to do with a man or place which never succeeds, because, although a man may appear to be honest and intelligent, yet if he tries this or that thing and always fails, it is on account of some fault or infirmity that you may not be able to discover but nevertheless which must exist.

There is no such thing in the world as luck. There never was a man who could go out in the morning and find a purse full of gold in the street to-day, and another to-morrow, and so on, day after day: He may do so once in his life; but so far as mere luck is concerned, he is as liable to lose it as to find it. "Like causes produce like effects." If a man adopts the proper methods to be successful, "luck" will not prevent him. If he does not succeed, there are reasons for it, although, perhaps, he may not be able to see them.

There are so many great points in this chapter. PT Barnum circles back again to what makes someone successful in getting money (sales)...he's willing to work, he seeks to understand and know what is involved in his work, and he continues to work day in and day out to make money in business. The poor man doesn't learn enough or do enough to make it. Love to learn.

Be cautious AND bold is a great balance to strike. Being too cautious keeps you from moving forward. Being too bold becomes reckless. In sales, prospects on either end of the spectrum can be a challenge. Sales people need to strike this balance as well so they can deal with the prospect's emotions. The same is true in celebration or defeat. Stay even and calm.

There is a deep commitment to do something with all your might. That's 100% commitment on every level. "Well, I don't know if I want to do that", or "This isn't that easy, maybe it's not worth it." doesn't pay bills. Here he notes, whatever you do, meaning everything you do, do it with all your might. You need to be committed completely with everything large and small.

Successful entrepreneurs have this work ethic. They are steady and strong, like a marathon runner has to be. They are in for the long run not the short sprint. Sometimes people don't realize how much work goes into becoming an "overnight" success. It's years of deliberate action, repetitive tasks, laser focus, tough skin, and relentless pursuit. You can do this!

CHAPTER FIVE

Secret 3
Don't Get Above Your Business
- PT Barnum

Young men after they get through their business training, or apprenticeship, instead of pursuing their avocation and rising in their business, will often lie about doing nothing. They say; "I have learned my business, but I am not going to be a hireling; what is the object of learning my trade or profession, unless I establish myself?"'

"Have you capital to start with?"

"No, but I am going to have it."

"How are you going to get it?"

"I will tell you confidentially; I have a wealthy old aunt, and she will die pretty soon; but if she does not, I expect to find some rich old man who will lend me a few thousands to give me a start. If I only get the money to start with I will do well."

There is no greater mistake than when a young man believes he will succeed with borrowed money. Why? Because every man's experience coincides with that of Mr. Astor, who said, "it was more difficult for him to accumulate his first thousand dollars, than all the succeeding millions that made up his colossal fortune." Money is good for nothing unless you know the value of it by experience. Give a boy twenty thousand dollars and put him in business, and the chances are that he will lose every dollar of it before he is a year older. Like buying a ticket in the lottery; and drawing a prize, it is "easy come, easy go." He does not know the value of it; nothing is worth anything, unless it costs effort. Without self-denial and economy; patience and perseverance, and commencing with capital which you have not earned, you are not sure to succeed in accumulating. Young men, instead of "waiting for dead men's shoes," should be up and doing, for there is no class of persons who are so unaccommodating in regard to dying as these rich old people, and it is fortunate for the expectant heirs that it is so. Nine out of ten of the rich men of our country to-day, started out in life as poor boys, with determined wills, industry, perseverance, economy and good habits. They went on gradually, made their own money and saved it; and this is the best way to acquire a fortune. Stephen Girard started life as a poor cabin boy, and died worth nine million dollars. A.T. Stewart was a poor Irish boy; and he paid taxes on a million and a half dollars of income, per year. John Jacob Astor was a poor farmer boy, and died worth twenty millions. Cornelius Vanderbilt began life rowing a boat from Staten Island to New York; he presented our government with a steamship worth a million of dollars, and died worth fifty million. "There is no royal road to learning," says the proverb, and I may say it is equally true, "there is no royal road to wealth." But I think there is a royal road to both. The road to learning is a royal one; the road that enables the student to expand his intellect and add every day to his stock of knowledge, until, in the pleasant process of intellectual growth, he is able to solve the most profound problems, to count the stars, to analyze every atom of the globe, and to measure the firmament this is a regal highway, and it is the only road worth traveling.

So in regard to wealth. Go on in confidence, study the rules, and above all things, study human nature; for "the proper study of mankind is man," and you will find that while expanding the intellect and the muscles, your enlarged experience will enable you every day to accumulate more and more principal, which will increase itself by interest and otherwise, until you arrive at a state of independence. You will find, as a general thing, that the poor boys get rich and the rich boys get poor. For instance, a rich man at his decease, leaves a large estate to his family. His eldest sons, who have helped him earn his fortune, know by experience the value of money; and they take their inheritance and add to it. The separate portions of the young children are placed at interest, and the little fellows are patted on the head, and told a dozen times a day, "you are rich; you will never have to work, you can always have whatever you wish, for you were born with a golden spoon in your mouth." The young heir soon finds out what that means; he has the finest dresses and playthings; he is crammed with sugar candies and almost "killed with kindness," and he passes from school to school, petted and flattered. He becomes arrogant and self-conceited, abuses his teachers, and carries everything with a high hand. He knows nothing of the real value of money, having never earned any; but he knows all about the "golden spoon" business. At college, he invites his poor fellow-students to his room, where he "wines and dines" them. He is cajoled and caressed, and called a glorious good follow, because he is so lavish of his money. He gives his game suppers, drives his fast horses, invites his chums to fetes and parties, determined to have lots of "good times." He spends the night in frolics and debauchery, and leads off his companions with the familiar song, "we won't go home till morning." He gets them to join him in pulling down signs, taking gates from their hinges and throwing them into back yards and horse-ponds. If the police arrest them, he knocks them down, is taken to the lockup, and joyfully foots the bills.

"Ah! my boys," he cries, "what is the use of being rich, if you can't enjoy yourself?"

He might more truly say, "if you can't make a fool of yourself;" but he is "fast," hates slow things, and doesn't "see it." Young men loaded down with other people's money are almost sure to lose all they inherit, and they acquire all sorts of bad habits which, in the majority of cases, ruin them in health, purse and character. In this country, one generation follows another, and the poor of to-day are rich in the next generation, or the third. Their experience leads them on, and they become rich, and they leave vast riches to their young children. These children, having been reared in luxury, are inexperienced and get poor; and after long experience another generation comes on and gathers up riches again in turn. And thus "history repeats itself," and happy is he who by listening to the experience of others avoids the rocks and shoals on which so many have been wrecked.

"In England, the business makes the man." If a man in that country is a mechanic or working-man, he is not recognized as a gentleman. On the occasion of my first appearance before Queen Victoria, the Duke of Wellington asked me what sphere in life General Tom Thumb's parents were in.

"His father is a carpenter," I replied.

"Oh! I had heard he was a gentleman," was the response of His Grace.

In this Republican country, the man makes the business. No matter whether he is a blacksmith, a shoemaker, a farmer, banker or lawyer, so long as his business is legitimate, he may be a gentleman. So any "legitimate" business is a double blessing it helps the man engaged in it, and also helps others. The Farmer supports his own family, but he also benefits the merchant or mechanic who needs the products of his farm. The tailor not only makes a living by his trade, but he also benefits the farmer, the clergyman and others who cannot make their own clothing. But all these classes often may be gentlemen.

The great ambition should be to excel all others engaged in the same occupation.

The college-student who was about graduating, said to an old lawyer:

"I have not yet decided which profession I will follow. Is your profession full?"

"The basement is much crowded, but there is plenty of room up-stairs," was the witty and truthful reply.

No profession, trade, or calling, is overcrowded in the upper story. Wherever you find the most honest and intelligent merchant or banker, or the best lawyer, the best doctor, the best clergyman, the best shoemaker, carpenter, or anything else, that man is most sought for, and has always enough to do. As a nation, Americans are too superficial—they are striving to get rich quickly, and do not generally do their business as substantially and thoroughly as they should, but whoever excels all others in his own line, if his habits are good and his integrity undoubted, cannot fail to secure abundant patronage, and the wealth that naturally follows. Let your motto then always be "Excelsior," for by living up to it there is no such word as fail.

It's an interesting observation that the poor become rich and the rich become poor because of how they understand the value of money and what it takes to earn it. Owning a business is a noble trade because of what it provides for others in addition to the owner and the owner's family. Even back then people wanted to get rich quick and take short cuts.

If you look at a lot of the most successful entrepreneurs today, a lot of them started the same way they did back more than a century ago...*Nine out of ten rich men of our country to-day, started out in life as poor boys, with determined wills, industry, perseverance, economy and good habits.* They weren't above their business. They were in it, working and growing it.

I was raised in an upper middle class family. I didn't miss a meal. I wasn't worried about having a roof over my head or if I could get clothes for school. My desire to have money in my life wasn't the same as the person who was raised without the basics. The struggle of being poor wasn't in my upbringing. If you are rich or poor, success comes from good habits as he says.

Those good habits make up someone's character. If you look at sales success through this lense, it is the person who is focused, resourceful, educated about their industry, determined, and disciplined in their habits that become successful. Every successful business person I know has those traits. They are constantly learning and can figure out how things need to work.

CHAPTER SIX

Secret 4
Be Systematic - PT Barnum

Men should be systematic in their business. A person who does business by rule, having a time and place for everything, doing his work promptly, will accomplish twice as much and with half the trouble of him who does it carelessly and slipshod. By introducing system into all your transactions, doing one thing at a time, always meeting appointments with punctuality, you find leisure for pastime and recreation; whereas the man who only half does one thing, and then turns to something else, and half does that, will have his business at loose ends, and will never know when his day's work is done, for it never will be done. Of course, there is a limit to all these rules. We must try to preserve the happy medium, for there is such a thing as being too systematic. There are men and women, for instance, who put away things so carefully that they can never find them again. It is too much like the "red tape" formality at Washington, and Mr. Dickens' "Circumlocution Office,"—all theory and no result.

When the "Astor House" was first started in New York city, it was undoubtedly the best hotel in the country. The proprietors had learned a good deal in Europe regarding hotels, and the landlords were proud of the rigid system which pervaded every department of their great establishment. When twelve o'clock at night had arrived, and there were a number of guests around, one of the proprietors would say, "Touch that bell, John;" and in two minutes sixty servants, with a water-bucket in each hand, would present themselves in the hall. "This," said the landlord, addressing his guests, "is our fire-bell; it will show you we are quite safe here; we do everything systematically." This was before the Croton water was introduced into the city. But they sometimes carried their system too far. On one occasion, when the hotel was thronged with guests, one of the waiters was suddenly indisposed, and although there were fifty waiters in the hotel, the landlord thought he must have his full complement, or his "system" would be interfered with. Just before dinner-time, he rushed down stairs and said, "There must be another waiter, I am one waiter short, what can I do?" He happened to see "Boots," the Irishman. "Pat," said he, "wash your hands and face; take that white apron and come into the dining-room in five minutes." Presently Pat appeared as required, and the proprietor said: "Now Pat, you must stand behind these two chairs, and wait on the gentlemen who will occupy them; did you ever act as a waiter?"

"I know all about it, sure, but I never did it."

Like the Irish pilot, on one occasion when the captain, thinking he was considerably out of his course, asked, "Are you certain you understand what you are doing?"

Pat replied, "Sure and I knows every rock in the channel."

That moment, "bang" thumped the vessel against a rock.

"Ah! be-jabers, and that is one of 'em," continued the pilot. But to return to the dining-room. "Pat," said the landlord, "here we do everything systematically. You must first give the gentlemen each a plate of soup, and when they finish that, ask them what they will have next."

Pat replied, "Ah! an' I understand parfectly the vartues of shystem."

Very soon in came the guests. The plates of soup were placed before them. One of Pat's two gentlemen ate his soup; the other did not care for it. He said: "Waiter, take this plate away and bring me some fish." Pat looked at the untasted plate of soup, and remembering the *instructions of the landlord in regard to "system," replied: "Not till ye have ate yer supe!"*

Of course that was carrying "system" entirely too far.

Every successful business has systems. The most famous example that comes to my mind is the story of McDonald's. The original brothers who opened the first McDonalds had systems for everything so they could be more efficient. What they did was revolutionary for the restaurant business. Those same systems are what make McDonalds the success it is today.

Today a lot of business systems are automated with technology. Every business should have a sales system as well, whatever that is for you. Without a system, your sales will suffer, especially if you have a sales team all doing whatever they think works best for them. There is a process to every success and every achievement. Repeat that process and you will get results.

The contrast of the person with a system and one without is really about being organized and staying focused. All successful entrepreneurs have ways of staying organized and getting things done. They create their own systems to keep track of things and anticipate what is going to be needed. When I organize my work and use a system, I am always successful.

His analogy of the sea captain hitting a rock in the channel reminded me of the Titanic sinking. JT Barnum lived from 1810 - 1891. The titanic sunk in 1912 hitting an iceberg in the ocean. When we think we know what we're doing but don't know what is up ahead, we can get in trouble. We need to have systems in place to keep us on track. It's a way to navigate a course.

CHAPTER SEVEN

Secret 5
Advertise Your Business
- PT Barnum

We all depend, more or less, upon the public for our support. We all trade with the public—lawyers, doctors, shoemakers, artists, blacksmiths, showmen, opera stagers, railroad presidents, and college professors. Those who deal with the public must be careful that their goods are valuable; that they are genuine, and will give satisfaction. When you get an article which you know is going to please your customers, and that when they have tried it, they will feel they have got their money's worth, then let the fact be known that you have got it. Be careful to advertise it in some shape or other because it is evident that if a man has ever so good an article for sale, and nobody knows it, it will bring him no return. In a country like this, where nearly everybody reads, and where newspapers are issued and circulated in editions of five thousand to two hundred thousand, it would be very unwise if this channel was not taken advantage of to reach the public in advertising. A newspaper goes into the family, and is read by wife and children, as well as the head of the home; hence hundreds and thousands of people may read your advertisement, while you are attending to your routine business. Many, perhaps, read it while you are asleep. The whole philosophy of life is, first "sow," then "reap." That is the way the farmer does; he plants his potatoes and corn, and sows his grain, and then goes about something else, and the time comes when he reaps. But he never reaps first and sows afterwards. This principle applies to all kinds of business, and to nothing more eminently than to advertising. If a man has a genuine article, there is no way in which he can reap more advantageously than by "sowing" to the public in this way. He must, of course, have a really good article, and one which will please his customers; anything spurious will not succeed permanently because the public is wiser than many imagine. Men and women are selfish, and we all prefer purchasing where we can get the most for our money and we try to find out where we can most surely do so.

You may advertise a spurious article, and induce many people to call and buy it once, but they will denounce you as an impostor and swindler, and your business will gradually die out and leave you poor. This is right. Few people can safely depend upon chance custom. You all need to have your customers return and purchase again. A man said to me, "I have tried advertising and did not succeed; yet I have a good article."

I replied, "My friend, there may be exceptions to a general rule. But how do you advertise?"

"I put it in a weekly newspaper three times, and paid a dollar and a half for it." I replied: "Sir, advertising is like learning—'a little is a dangerous thing!'"

A French writer says that "The reader of a newspaper does not see the first mention of an ordinary advertisement; the second insertion he sees, but does not read; the third insertion he reads; the fourth insertion, he looks at the price; the fifth insertion, he speaks of it to his wife; the sixth insertion, he is ready to purchase, and the seventh insertion, he purchases." Your object in advertising is to make the public understand what you have got to sell, and if you have not the pluck to keep advertising, until you have imparted that information, all the money you have spent is lost. You are like the fellow who told the *gentleman if he would give him ten cents it would save him a dollar. "How can I help you so much with so small a sum?" asked the gentleman in surprise. "I started out this morning (hiccuped the fellow) with the full determination to get drunk, and I have spent my only dollar to accomplish the object, and it has not quite done it. Ten cents worth more of whiskey would just do it, and in this manner I should save the dollar already expended."*

So a man who advertises at all must keep it up until the public know who and what he is, and what his business is, or else the money invested in advertising is lost.

Some men have a peculiar genius for writing a striking advertisement, one that will arrest the attention of the reader at first sight. This fact, of course, gives the advertiser a great advantage. Sometimes a man makes himself popular by an unique sign or a curious display in his window, recently I observed a swing sign extending over the sidewalk in front of a store, on which was the inscription in plain letters.

Things were so simple back when PT Barnum lived. Advertising was done in newspapers, which everyone read. Now there are so many options to choose from. One thing hasn't changed...your customers need to know about you and your products or services. If they don't know you, they won't buy from you. Advertising is sowing and getting the sale is reaping.

He points to something else here that advertisers have known for over 120 years. A customer won't buy until the 7th time they've seen your ad or store or product or post. People haven't changed that much. So you need to stay in front of people with what you have to offer. And if you give up advertising before you've done enough of it, your efforts will be wasted.

Very successful entrepreneurs know that who ever can spend the most money on advertising wins. Big corporations know that whoever spends the most money on advertising wins. Back in the 1980's when I worked in media, there was a media coffee war when a top brand increased it's ad spend. Everyone in the category followed suit.

With the internet and so many options for consumers to get what they need, a business needs to find creative ways to advertise what they are doing. There are a lot of FREE ways to get the word out with social media and get organic exposure as well. But, the biggest success stories, the most well known entrepreneurs are well known because they spend money on ads.

CHAPTER EIGHT

Secret 6
Be Polite And Kind To Your Customers - PT Barnum

Politeness and civility are the best capital ever invested in business. Large stores, gilt signs, flaming advertisements, will all prove unavailing if you or your employees treat your patrons abruptly. The truth is, the more kind and liberal a man is, the more generous will be the patronage bestowed upon him. "Like begets like." The man who gives the greatest amount of goods of a corresponding quality for the least sum (still reserving for himself a profit) will generally succeed best in the long run. This brings us to the golden rule, "As ye would that men should do to you, do ye also to them" and they will do better by you than if you always treated them as if you wanted to get the most you could out of them for the least return. Men who drive sharp bargains with their customers, acting as if they never expected to see them again, will not be mistaken. They will never see them again as customers. People don't like to pay and get kicked also.

One of the ushers in my Museum once told me he intended to whip a man who was in the lecture-room as soon as he came out.

"What for?" I inquired.

"Because he said I was no gentleman," replied the usher.

"Never mind," I replied, "he pays for that, and you will not convince him you are a gentleman by whipping him. I cannot afford to lose a customer. If you whip him, he will never visit the Museum again, and he will induce friends to go with him to other places of amusement instead of this, and thus you see, I should be a serious loser."

"But he insulted me," muttered the usher.

"Exactly," I replied, "and if he owned the Museum, and you had paid him for the privilege of visiting it, and he had then insulted you, there might be some reason in your resenting it, but in this instance he is the man who pays, while we receive, and you must, therefore, put up with his bad manners."

My usher laughingly remarked, that this was undoubtedly the true policy; but he added that he should not object to an increase of salary if he was expected to be abused in order to promote my interest.

Customer service is still about the customer. It's very rare that a business has a product that is so good that the proprietor can treat people rudely and have them come back. People remember how you made them feel. People can be extreme loyalists and huge fans when they are treated right and they love your products. They will tell everyone they know.

Customer experience is something that certain industries are really good at. Other industries, not so much. If you want to grow your business, take care of your customers, offer a quality product, and stand behind what you do. When you do more than what is expected and people get tremendous value when they get results, you will be in business for a long time.

Customer experience is so important that companies create campaigns around what customer experience they are providing. Disneyland is the happiest place on earth. BMW is the ultimate driving machine. There is a reason companies spend so much time and money creating campaigns to evoke a feeling of great customer experience so people make a purchase.

Be polite and kind to your customers is something that entrepreneurs need to ensure is happening in how they do things and how their staff does things. Your sales team is the first impression your potential customers will have of your business. Businesses that don't focus on customer experience have to work a lot harder to keep their doors open.

CHAPTER NINE

Secret 7
The Mind Of The Salesman
– William Walker Atkinson

The mental qualities most requisite to the Salesman may be stated as follows:

1. Self Respect. It is important to the Salesman that he cultivate the faculty of Self Respect. By this we do not mean egotism, conceit, superciliousness, imperiousness, hauteur, snobbishness, etc., all of which are detrimental qualities. Self Respect, on the contrary imparts the sense of rue manhood or womanhood, self-reliance, dignity, courage and independence...... Learn to look the world in the eyes without flinching. Throw off the fear of the crowd, and the impression that you are unworthy. Learn to believe in yourself, and to respect yourself. Let your motto be "I Can; I Will; I Dare; I Do!"

One's physical carriage and attitude tends to react upon his own mental attitude as well as also impressing those in whose presence he is. There is always an action and reaction between mind and body. Just as mental states take form in physical actions, so do physical actions react upon the mind and influence mental states. Frown continually and you will feel cross; smile and you will feel cheerful. Carry yourself like a man, and you will feel like a man. Carl H. Pierce says regarding the proper carriage of a salesman: "Remember that you are asking no favors; that you have nothing to apologize for, and that you have every reason in the world to hold your head up high. And it is wonderful what this holding of the head will do in the way of increasing sales. We have seen salesmen get entrance to the offices of Broadway buyers simply through the holding of the head straight up from the shoulders. The rule to follow is: Have your ear lobes directly over your shoulders, so that a plumb line hung from the ears describes the line of your body. Be sure not to carry the head either to the right or left but vertical. Many men make the mistake, especially when waiting for a prospect to finish some important piece of business, of leaning the head either to the right or left. This indicates weakness. A study of men discloses the fact that the strong men never tilt the head. Their heads sit perfectly straight on strong necks. Their shoulders, held easily yet firmly in correct position, are inspiring in their strength indicating poise. Every line of the body, in other words, denotes the thought of the bearer."

So cultivate not only the inner sense of Self Respect, but also the outward indications of that mental state. Thus do you secure the benefit of the action and reaction between body and mind.

II. Poise. The salesman should cultivate Poise, which manifests in balance, tranquility and ease. Poise is that mental quality which maintains a natural balance between the various faculties, feelings, emotions and tendencies.…..... Poise enables one to correctly balance himself, mentally, instead of allowing his feelings or emotions to run away with him….....Poise enables one to "keep himself well in hand." The man who has Poise indeed has Power, for he is never thrown off his balance, and consequently always remains master of the situation. Did you ever hear of, or see, the Gyroscope? Well, it is a peculiar little mechanical contrivance consisting of a whirling wheel within a frame work, the peculiarity consisting of the arrangement and action of the wheel which by its motion always maintains its balance and equilibrium. No matter how the little apparatus is turned, it always maintains its equilibrium. It is likely to play an important part in aerial navigation and mono-rail systems of transportation, in the future.

Well, here is the point—be a Mental Gyroscope. Cultivate the mental quality which acts automatically in the direction of keeping your balance and centre of mental gravity. This does not mean that you should be a prig, or a solemn-faced smug bore..... On the contrary, always be natural in manner and action. The point is to always maintain your balance, and mental control, instead of allowing your feelings or emotions to run away with you. Poise means Mastery—lack of it means Slavery. As Edward Carpenter says: "How rare indeed to meet a man! How common rather to discover a creature hounded on by tyrant thoughts (or cares, or desires), cowering, wincing under the lash—or perchance priding himself to run merrily in obedience to a driver that rattles the reins and persuades himself that he is free." Poise is the Mental Gyroscope—keep it in good working order.

III. Cheerfulness. The "bright, cheerful and happy" mental attitude.... is a magnet of success to the salesman. The "grouch" is the negative pole of personality, and does more to repel people than almost any other quality. So much in demand is the cheerful demeanor and mental state, that people often give undue preference to those possessing it, and pass over a "grouchy" individual of merit in favor of the man of less merit but who possesses the "sunshine" in his personality. The "man with the southern exposure" is in demand. There is enough in the world to depress people without having gloom thrust upon them by persons calling to sell goods. Well has the poet said:

"Laugh, and the world laughs with you;
Weep, and you weep alone.
For this sad old earth is in need of mirth;
It has troubles enough of its own."

The world prefers "Happy Jim" to "Gloomy Gus," and will bestow its favors upon the first while turning a cold shoulder to the second. The Human Wet Blanket is not a welcome guest, while the individual who manages to "let a little sunshine in" upon all occasions is always welcome. The optimistic and cheerful spirit creates for itself an atmosphere which, perhaps unconsciously, diffuses itself in all places visited by the individual. Cheerfulness is contagious, and is a most valuable asset. We have known individuals whose sunny exteriors caused a relief in the tension on the part of those whom they visited. We have heard it said of such people: "I am always glad to see that fellow—he brightens me up." This does not mean that one should endeavor to become a professional wit, a clown, or a comedian—that is not the point. The idea underlying this mental state and attribute of personality is Cheerfulness, and a disposition to look on the bright side of things, and to manifest that mental state as the sun does its rays. Learn to radiate Cheerfulness. It is not so much a matter of saying things, as it is a matter of thinking them. A man's inner thoughts are reflected in his outward personality.

So cultivate the inner Cheerfulness before you can hope to manifest its outer characteristics. There is nothing so pitiful, or which falls so flat, as a counterfeit Cheerfulness—it is worse than the minstrel jokes of the last decade. To be cheerful one does not have to be a "funny man." The atmosphere of true Cheerfulness can proceed only from within. The higher-class Japanese instruct their children to maintain a cheerful demeanor and a smiling face no matter what happens, even though the heart is breaking. They consider this the obligation of their caste, and regard it as most unworthy of the person, as well as insulting to others, to manifest any other demeanor or expression. Their theory, which forms a part of their wonderful code called "Bushido," is that it is an impertinence to obtrude one's grief, sorrow, misfortunes, or "grouch," upon others. They reserve for their own inner circle their sorrows and pains, and always present a cheerful and bright appearance to others. The Salesman would do well to remember the "Bushido,"—he needs it in his business. Avoid the "grouch" mental state as you would a pestilence. Don't be a "knocker"—for "knocks," like chickens, come home to roost, bringing their chicks with them.

IV. Politeness. Courtesy is a valuable asset to a Salesman. Not only this, but it is a trait characteristic of gentlemen in all walks of life, and is a duty toward oneself as well as toward others. By politeness and courtesy we do not mean the formal, artificial outward acts and remarks which are but the counterfeit of the real thing, but, instead, that respectful demeanor toward others which is the mark of innate refinement and good-breeding. Courtesy and politeness do not necessarily consist of formal rules of etiquette, but of an inner sympathy and understanding of others which manifests in a courteous demeanor toward them. Everyone likes to be treated with appreciation and understanding and is willing to repay the same in like form. One does not need to be a raw "jollier" in order to be polite. Politeness—true politeness—comes from within, and it is almost impossible to imitate it successfully. Its spirit may be expressed by the idea of trying to see the good in everyone and then acting toward the person as if his good were in plain evidence. Give to those with whom you come in contact the manner, attention and respect to which they would be entitled if they were actually manifesting the highest good within them.

One of the best retail salesmen we ever knew attributed his success to his ability to "get on the customer's side of the counter," that is, to try to see the matter from the customer's viewpoint. This led to a sympathetic understanding which was most valuable. If the Salesman can manage to put himself in the place of the customer, he may see things with a new light, and thus gain an understanding of the customer which will enable him, the Salesman, to manifest a true politeness toward his customers. But politeness and courtesy does not mean a groveling, cringing attitude of mind or demeanor. True politeness and courtesy must have as its background and support, Self Respect.

Allied to politeness is the quality called Tact, which is defined as the "peculiar skill or adroitness in doing or saying exactly that which is required by, or is suited to, the circumstances; nice perception or discernment." A little consideration will show that Tact must depend upon an understanding of the viewpoint and mental attitude of the other person, so that if one has the key to the one he may open the door of the other. An understanding of the other person's position, and an application of the true spirit of politeness, will go a long way toward establishing the quality of tactfulness. Tact is a queer combination of Worldly Wisdom and the Golden Rule—a mixture of the ability to seek into the other person's mind, and the ability to speak unto others as you would that others speak unto you, under the same circumstances. The trait called Adaptability, or the faculty of adjusting oneself to conditions, and to the personality of others, also belongs to this category. Adaptability depends upon the ability to see the other person's position. As a writer says: "Those individuals who are out of harmony with their surroundings disappear to make room for those who are in harmony with them." When the keynote of the understanding of the minds of others is found, the whole subject of true politeness, tact and adaptability is understood and may be applied in practice.

I did some editing on this chapter because it's long but also because there is some metaphysical stuff that isn't necessarily for everyone. There are a lot of things that successful entrepreneurs do that are included in this chapter. Their appearance, their stature, their mental discipline, kindness, and charisma are a deliberate focus in how they operate.

He talks about self respect in the beginning. Confidence is another way to look at self respect when it comes to sales. When you get on sales calls, you have to be confident about yourself and what you're talking about. If you've ever dealt with a salesperson that didn't have confidence or self respect, you probably didn't buy from them unless you needed what they had.

His discussion about how your carry your body is another point that has a lot of merit. Studies have been done about this. How a person sits in a chair while they are at their desk will impact how they feel and their job performance. If you find you're a person who tilts your head a lot, practice in a mirror so you know what it feels like to keep your head straight on your neck.

If you do face to face sales, be sure you're not raising your eyebrows a lot and scrunching your forehead. It doesn't look good and can be distracting. I watched a video of myself when I was interviewed on a cable show when I was doing music in Colorado. I was scrunching my forehead when I talked. It looked terrible. I had to practice a lot in the mirror to stop doing it.

Cheerfulness is a must in sales. Upbeat people close more deals. It's great to see this written in 1912. It shows us that people at the core of who they are haven't changed much. Entrepreneurs need to understand how they are presenting themselves in the market. In sales, you have to be a bright spot in someone's day or they won't want to buy from you. It's so important.

Politeness is also mentioned here for the salesman. I would say this one can be challenging for people at times. We are living in a time of instant access, instant gratification, and lots of distractions. Politeness isn't at the forefront of a lot of people's minds. Successful entrepreneurs have politeness mastered. They know politeness keeps customers coming back.

Here are some more points he discusses about the mind of the salesman in his next chapter…

VI. Hope. The Salesman should cultivate the Optimistic Outlook upon Life. He should encourage the earnest expectation of the good things to come, and move forward to the realization thereof. Much of life success depends upon the mental attitude of, and the confident expectation of, a successful outcome. Earnest Desire, Confident Expectation, and Resolute Action—this is the threefold key of attainment. Thought manifests itself in action, and we grow in accordance with the mental pattern or mould we create for ourselves. If you will look around you you will find that the men who have succeeded, and who are succeeding, are those who have maintained the hopeful mental attitude—who have always looked forward to the star of hope even in the moments of the greatest trouble and temporary reverses. If a man loses his hope permanently he is defeated. Hope is the incentive which is always drawing man onward and upward. Hope backed by Will and Determination is almost invincible. Learn to look on the bright side of things, to believe in your ultimate success. Learn to look upward and forward—heed the motto, "look aloft!" Cultivate the "rubber-ball spirit," by which you will be able to bounce higher up the harder you are thrown down. There is a subtle psychological law by the operation of which we tend to materialize our ideals. The "confident expectation" backed by actions will win out in the end. Hitch your wagon to the Star of Hope.

VII. Enthusiasm. Very few people understand the true meaning of the word "enthusiasm," although they may use it quite frequently in ordinary conversation. Enthusiasm means far more than energy, activity, interest and hope—it means the expression of the "soul" in mental and physical actions. The Greeks used the word as meaning "inspiration; moved by the gods," from which arose the later meaning of "inspired by a superhuman or divine power." The modern usage is defined as: "Enkindled and kindling fervor of the soul; ardent and imaginative zeal or interest; lively manifestation of joy or zeal;" etc. A person filled with enthusiasm seems to move and act from the very centre of his being—that part which we mean when we say "soul." There is a wonderful power in rightly directed enthusiasm, which serves not only to arouse within one his full powers, but also tends to impress others in the direction of mental contagion. Mental states are contagious, and enthusiasm is one of the most active of mental states. Enthusiasm comes nearer to being "soul-power" than any other outward expression of mental states. It is allied to the soul-stirring impulse of music, poetry, and the drama. We can feel it in the words of a writer, speaker, orator, preacher, singer or poet. Enthusiasm may be analyzed as Inspired Interest. As Walter D. Moody says: "It will be found that all men possessed of personal magnetism are very much in earnest. Their intense earnestness is magnetic." The best authorities agree that Enthusiasm is the active principle of what has been called Personal Magnetism.

........Some of us are magnetic—others not. Some of us are warm, attractive, love-inspiring and friendship-making, while others are cold, intellectual, thoughtful, reasoning, but not magnetic. Let a learned man of the latter type address an audience and it will soon tire of his intellectual discourse, and will manifest symptoms of drowsiness. He talks at them, but not into them—he makes them think, not feel, which is most tiresome to the majority of persons, and few speakers succeed who attempt to merely make people think—they want to be made to feel. People will pay liberally to be made to feel or laugh, while they will begrudge a dime for instruction or talk that will make them think. Pitted against a learned man of the type mentioned above, let there be a half-educated, but very loving, ripe and mellow man, with but nine-tenths of the logic and erudition of the first man, yet such a man carries along his crowd with perfect ease, and everybody is wide-awake, treasuring up every good thing that falls from his lips. The reasons are palpable and plain. It is heart against head; soul against logic; and soul is bound to win every time." And as Newman says: "Deductions have no power of persuasion. The heart is commonly reached, not through the reason, but through the imagination, by means of direct impressions, by the testimony of facts and events, by history, by description. Persons influence us, looks subdue us, deeds inflame us." Enthusiasm imparts that peculiar quality that we call "life," which constitutes such an important part in the personality of a salesman. Remember we have analyzed enthusiasm as inspired earnestness—think over this analysis, and grasp its inner meaning. The very word "enthusiasm" is inspiring—visualize it and let it incite you to its expression when you feel "dead." The very thought of it is a stimulant!

VIII. Determination. The Salesman needs the quality of dogged determination, persistence, and "stick-to-itiveness." This bulldog quality must be developed. The "I Can and I Will" spirit must be cultivated. Determination is composed of several constituent faculties.

First comes Combativeness or the quality of "tackling" obstacles. This is a marked quality in all strong characters. It manifests as courage, boldness, resistance, opposition, and disposition to combat opposition rather than to yield to it.

Allied to this faculty is another which bears the very inadequate name of Destructiveness, which expresses itself in the direction of breaking down barriers, pushing aside obstacles, making headway; pushing to the front; holding one's own; etc. It is the quality of the man who makes his own paths and builds up his own trade. It is the "pioneer" faculty of the mind which clears away the ground, lays foundations and builds the first log-cabin.

Then comes Continuity, the faculty which is well-defined as "stick-to-itiveness," which enables one to stick to his task until it is finished. This faculty gives stability and staying qualities, and enables a man to finish well. The lack of this quality often neutralizes the work of other good faculties, causing the person to "let go" too soon, and to thus lose the fruits of his labors.

Finally, comes the faculty of Firmness, which gives to one the quality of tenacity, perseverance, fixity, decision and stability, accompanied by a certain "stubborn tendency" which holds the other faculties together. A certain amount of this quality of "jackass courage" is needed in the mental make up of a Salesman. If a person is 'set' to a certain extent it enables him to maintain his position without the constant wear and tear upon his will that is met with by those lacking it. This faculty prevents one from being "sidetracked," and enables him to "put his hand to the plow and look not backward." It holds the chisel of the will up against the metal of circumstances until the work is accomplished. It enables one to be like the rock against which harmlessly beat the waves of opposition and competition. It enables one to see his object, and then to march straight to it.

So much of success in sales and in life has to do with mindset. Just about every mentor, teacher, and prominent person talking about success will at some point discuss the mindset of success. Hope is at the core of having a great mindset. I love what he says...the *"rubber-ball spirit," by which you will be able to bounce higher up the harder you are thrown down.*

His talk on enthusiasm touches on a number of things true today. People wonder why some people succeed and some don't. Someone who operates from their heart is more influential than someone who operates from knowledge. The passion of a salesperson is what people like to experience when they buy. Steve Jobs was a master of this introducing new Apple products.

His point about what people pay for.... to feel and laugh is spot on. It's good to know that when you want to connect with new customers. The heart is reached with imagination. A successful sales tactic used today takes the person into their pain, then talks about the dream they want to have (imagination), and then closes them on their solution to get there that costs a lot.

Determination is probably the most misunderstood aspect of success in sales for people just getting into it. PT Barnum titled it as perseverance. Successful people have a drive to get them to their goal that is not undermined by any kind of circumstance. The harder it is, the harder they dig in to get there. It's not for the faint at heart. To succeed in sales means not giving up.

I kind of feel that part of my success as a sales person/entrepreneur is refusing to not get what I want. To me, when I truly believe with all my heart that what I want is right and you tell me "No", I will find another way to explain to you so you say, "Yes". Thanks to my dad. And if you don't 'get it' the second time, I'll come back again. And I'll keep coming back so you can say, "Yes".

A successful entrepreneur/sales person, has a vision of something that is important for them to achieve. This isn't something insignificant. No one can have the kind of determination to succeed if their reason to succeed isn't extremely compelling. It's about your WHY. If your reason for doing something is weak, you won't stick with it long enough to succeed.

CHAPTER TEN

Secret 8
The Mind Of The Buyer
- William Walker Atkinson

While it is true that there is almost infinite variety among people, nevertheless, it is true that there are a few general classes into which the majority of buyers may be fitted or grouped for convenience. Let us now consider some of the more common classes, and see how the faculties, in combination, manifest themselves.

The Argumentive Buyer. This man finds his greatest pleasure in arguing, combating and disputing with the Salesman—argument for the sake of argument, not for the sake of truth or advantage. This trait arises from developed Combativeness and Destructiveness. Do not take these people too seriously. Let them enjoy a victory over you on minor points, and then after yielding gracefully coax them along the main lines of the selling talk. At the best, they are arguing over terms, definitions, forms, etc. and not over facts. Let them make their own definitions, terms and forms—and then take their order for the goods which you have fitted into their side of the argument. If, however, the argument is based upon true reasoning and with a legitimate intent, then reason with him calmly and respectfully.

The Conceited Buyer. This fellow is full of Approbativeness. We have told you about him elsewhere. Meet him on his own plane, and give him the particular bait indicated for his species—he will rise to it. Appearing to defer to him, you may work in your arguments and selling talk without opposition. Prefacing your explanation with "As you know by your own experience;" or "as your own good judgment has decided;" etc., you may tell your story without much opposition. You must always let him feel that you realize that you are in the presence of a great man.

The "Stone Wall" Buyer. This man has Self Esteem and Firmness largely developed. We have told you about him under those two headings. You must fly over, tunnel under, or walk around his stone wall of reserve and stubbornness. Let him keep his wall intact—he likes it, and it would be a shame to deprive him of it. A little careful search will generally show that he has left his flanks, or his rear unguarded. He will not let you in the front door—so go around to the kitchen door, or the side-door of the sitting room—they are not so well guarded.

The Irritable Buyer. This is an unpleasant combination of Approbativeness and Combativeness, in connection with poor digestion and disordered nerves. Do not quarrel with him, and let his manner slide over you like water off a duck's back. Stick to your selling talk, and above everything keep cool, confident, and speak in even tones. This course will tend to bring him down. If you show that you are not afraid of him, and cannot be made angry—if your tones are firm yet under control and not loud—he will gradually come down to meet you. If you lose your own temper, you may as well walk out. Simply ignore his "grouch"—deny it out of existence, as our New Thought friends would say.

The "Rough Shod" Buyer. This man has large Destructiveness, and Self Esteem, and wants to run things himself. He will try to ride rough shod over you. Keep cool, even-tempered, self-possessed, and firm yet respectful. Do not let him "rattle" you. It is often more of a "bluff" than anything else. Keep on "sawing wood;" and do not be scared off. These people are often but "lath-and-plaster" instead of the iron and steel they appear to be at first sight. Keep firm and calm, is the keynote in dealing with them.

The Cautious Buyer. This man generally has Cautiousness and Continuity well developed, and Hope deficient. He is conservative and fearful. Avoid frightening him with ideas of "new" things or "experiments." If you are selling new things or ideas, manage to blend them in with things with which he is familiar—associate the new and unfamiliar with the old and familiar. And be conservative and careful in your talk, do not give him the idea that you are a radical or a "new fangled idea" man. To him, be an "old fashioned person."

The Cunning Buyer. This fellow has large Secretiveness or Cunning—he belongs to the fox tribe. He likes to scheme out things for himself, so if you will content yourself with giving him broad hints, accompanied by expressive glances, regarding what can be done with your goods, he will be apt to scheme out something in that direction, and thinking he has done it all himself, he will be pleased and interested. Let him know that you appreciate his shrewdness, particularly if he shows that his Approbativeness is well developed. But, if not, better let him think that he is deceiving you regarding his true nature. The majority of cunning people, however, take pride in it, and relish a little grim appreciation of their quality.

The Dignified Buyer. This man has large Self Esteem, and probably also large Approbativeness. In either case, let him play the part for which Nature has cast him, and you play yours. Your part is in recognizing and respecting his dignity, by your manner and tone. Whether the dignity be real or assumed, a recognition of and falling in with it is appreciated and relished. Imagine that you are in the presence of your revered great-grandfather, or the bishop, and the rest will be easy. We once knew of a jovial, but indiscreet, salesman who lost a large sale to a buyer of this kind, by poking him in the ribs and calling him "old chap." The buyer barely escaped an attack of apoplexy—the Salesman entirely escaped a sale.

The "Mean" Buyer. This man is moved by Acquisitiveness. He is suspicious of you from the start, for he feels that you intend to get some money from him. Don't blame him—he's built that way. Instead, get his *mind off the subject and on to another, by plunging in at once with the statement that you have something upon which he can make money, or something that will save him money. Emphasize these points, and you will have aroused his curiosity. Then proceed along the same lines—something to make money for him, or something to save money for him—these are the only two arguments he can assimilate.*

The Intelligent Buyer. These people depend almost entirely upon reason and judgment. They are scarce. When you meet one of them, drop all attempts to play upon weak points, prejudices or feelings, and confine yourself strictly to logical and rational statements, presentation of your proposition, and argument thereon. Do not attempt sophistry, argument from false premises, or other fallacies. He will detect them at once, and will feel indignant. Talk straight from the shoulder, and confine yourself to facts, figures, principles, and logic.

I love this section of the book because at some point in everyone's experience in business, they will encounter these types of personalities. I was like a lot of these types of buyers when I was younger. What really changed me as a buyer was working in a high end department store in Beverly Hills. Customers saw me like a piece of furniture at best. It was a humbling time.

In our century, there are a number of personality types that have been categorized so we can deal with people effectively. Underlying all of it really goes back to what PT Barnum talked about also: Be polite and kind to people. When people are treated well, it's easier for them to behave well. If someone is mean and having a bad day, they need extra kindness. They are suffering.

CHAPTER ELEVEN

Secret 9
The Psychology Of Purchase
- William Walker Atkinson

There are several stages or phases manifested by the buyer in the mental process which results in a purchase. While it is difficult to state a hard and fast rule regarding the same, because of the variety of temperament, tendencies and mental habits possessed in several degrees by different individuals, still there are certain principles of feeling and thought manifested alike by each and every individual buyer, and a certain logical sequence is followed by all men in each and every original purchase. It follows, of course, that these principles, and this sequence, will be found to be operative in each and every original purchase, whether that purchase be the result of an advertisement, display of goods, recommendation, or the efforts of a salesman. The principle is the same in each and every case, and the sequence of the mental states is the same in each and every instance. Let us now consider these several mental states in their usual sequence.

The several mental states manifested by every buyer in an original purchase are given below in the order of sequence in which they are usually manifested:—

I.	Involuntary Attention.
II.	First Impression.
III.	Curiosity.
IV.	Associated Interest.
V.	Consideration.
VI.	Imagination.
VII.	Inclination.
VIII.	Deliberation.
IX.	Decision.
X.	Action.

We use the term "original purchase" in this connection in order to distinguish the original purchase from a repeated order or subsequent purchase of the same article, in which latter instance the mental process is far more simple and which consists merely in recognizing the inclination, or habit, and ordering the goods, without repeating the original complex mental operation. Let us now proceed to a consideration of the several mental stages of the original purchase, in logical sequence:—

I. Involuntary Attention. This mental state is the elementary phase of attention. Attention is not a faculty of the mind, but is instead the focusing of the consciousness upon one object to the temporary exclusion of all other objects. It is a turning of the mind on an object. The object of attention may be either external, such as a person or thing; or internal, such as a feeling, thought, memory, or idea. Attention may be either voluntary, that is, directed consciously by the will; or involuntary, that is, directed unconsciously and instinctively and apparently independently of the will. Voluntary attention is an acquired and developed power and is the attribute of the thinker, student and intellectual individual in all walks of life. Involuntary attention, on the contrary, is but little more than a reflex action, or a nervous response to some stimulus. As Halleck says: "Many persons scarcely get beyond the reflex stage. Any chance stimulus will take their attention away from their studies or their business." Sir William Hamilton made a still finer distinction, which is, however, generally overlooked by writers on the subject, but which is scientifically correct and which we shall follow in this book. He holds that there are three degrees or kinds of attention: (1) the reflex or involuntary, which is instinctive in nature; (2) that determined by desire or feeling, which partakes of both the involuntary and voluntary nature, and which although partly instinctive may be resisted by the will under the influence of the judgment; and (3) that determined by deliberate volition in response to reason, as in study, scientific games, rational deliberation, etc.

The first mental step of the purchase undoubtedly consists of involuntary or reflex attention, such as is aroused by a sudden sound, sight, or other sensation. The degree of this involuntary attention depends upon the intensity, suddenness, novelty, or movement of the object to which it responds. All persons respond to the stimuli arousing this form of attention, but in different degrees depending upon the preoccupation or concentration of the individual at the time. The striking or novel appearance of an advertisement; the window-display of goods; the appearance of the salesman—all these things instinctively arouse the involuntary attention, and the buyer "turns his mind on" them. But this turning the mind on belongs to Hamilton's first class— that of the instinctive response to the sight or sound, and not that aroused by desire or deliberate thought. It is the most elemental form of attention or mental effort, and to the salesman means simply: "Well, I see you!" Sometimes the prospect is so preoccupied or concentrated on other things that he barely "sees" the salesman until an added stimulus is given by a direct remark.

II. First Impression. This mental state is the hasty generalization resulting from the first impression of the object of attention—the advertisement, suggestion, display of goods, or the Salesman— depending in the last case upon the general appearance, action, manner, etc., as interpreted in the light of experience or association. In other words, the prospect forms a hasty general idea of the thing or person, either favorable or unfavorable, almost instinctively and unconsciously. The thing or person is associated or classed with others resembling it in the experience and memory of the prospect, and the result is either a good, bad or indifferent impression resulting from the suggestion of association. For this reason the ad. man and the window dresser endeavor to awaken favorable and pleasing associated memories and suggestions, and "puts his best foot foremost." The Salesman endeavors to do the same, and seeks to "put up a good front" in his Approach, in order to secure this valuable favorable first impression. People are influenced more than they will admit by these "first impressions," or suggestions, of appearance, manner, etc., and the man who understands psychology places great importance upon them. A favorable first impression smooths the way for the successful awakening of the later mental states. An unfavorable first impression, while it may be removed and remedied later, nevertheless is a handicap which the Salesman should avoid.

(Note: The mental process of the purchase now passes from the stage of involuntary attention, to that of attention inspired by desire and feeling which partakes of both the voluntary and involuntary elements. The first two stages of this form of attention are known as Curiosity and Associated Interest, respectively. In some cases Curiosity precedes, in others Associated Interest takes the lead, as we shall see. In other cases the manifestation of the two is almost simultaneous.)

III. Curiosity. This mental state is really a form of Interest, but is more elemental than Associated Interest, being merely the interest of novelty. It is the strongest item of interest in the primitive races, in children, and in many adults of elemental development and habits of thought. Curiosity is the form of Interest which is almost instinctive, and which impels one to turn the attention to strange and novel things. All animals possess it to a marked degree, as trappers have found out to their profit. Monkeys possess it to an inordinate degree, and the less developed individuals of the human race also manifest it to a highdegree. It is connected in some way with the primitive conditions of living things, and is probably a heritage from earlier and less secure conditions of living, where inquisitiveness regarding new, novel and strange sights and sounds was a virtue and the only means of acquiring experience and education. At any rate, there is certainly in human nature a decided instinctive tendency to explore the unknown and strange—the attraction of the mysterious; the lure of the secret things; the tantalizing call of the puzzle; the fascination of the riddle.

The Salesman who can introduce something in his opening talk that will arouse Curiosity in the prospect has done much to arouse his attention and interest. The street-corner fakir, and the "barker" for the amusement-park show, understand this principle in human nature, and appeal largely to it. They will blindfold a boy or girl, or will make strange motions or sounds, in order to arouse the curiosity of the crowd and to cause them to gather around—all this before the actual appeal to interest is made. In some buyers Curiosity precedes Associated Interest—the interest in the unknown and novel precedes the practical interest. In others the Associated Interest—the practical interest inspired by experience and association—precedes Curiosity, the latter manifesting simply as inquisitiveness regarding the details of the object which has aroused Associated Interest. In other cases, Curiosity and Associated Interest are so blended and shaded into each other that they act almost as one and simultaneously. On the whole, though, Curiosity is more elemental and crude than Associated Interest, and may readily be distinguished in the majority of cases.

IV. Associated Interest. This mental state is a higher form of interest than Curiosity. It is a practical interest in things relating to one's interests in life, his weal or woe, loves or hates, instead of being the mere interest in novelty of Curiosity. It is an acquired trait, while Curiosity is practically an instinctive trait. Acquired Interest develops with character, occupation, and education, while Curiosity manifests strongly in the very beginnings of character, and before education. Acquired Interest is manifested more strongly in the man of affairs, education and experience, while Curiosity has its fullest flower in the monkey, savage, young child and uncultured adult. Recognizing the relation between the two, it may be said that Curiosity is the root, and Associated Interest the flower.

Associated Interest depends largely upon the principle of Association or Apperception, the latter being defined as "that mental process by which the perceptions or ideas are brought into relation to our previous ideas and feelings, and thus are given a new clearness, meaning and application." Apperception is the mental process by which objects and ideas presented to us are perceived and thought of by us in the light of our past experience, temperament, tastes, likes and dislikes, occupation, interest, prejudices, etc., instead of as they actually are. We see everything through the colored glasses of our own personality and character. Halleck says of Apperception: "A woman may apperceive a passing bird as an ornament to her bonnet; a fruit grower, as an insect killer; a poet, as a songster; an artist, as a fine bit of coloring and form. The housewife may apperceive old rags as something to be thrown away; a ragpicker, as something to be gathered up. A carpenter, a botanist, an ornithologist, a hunter, and a geologist walking through a forest would not see the same things." The familiar tale of the text-books illustrates this principle. It relates that a boy climbed up a tree in a forest and watched the passers-by, and listened to their conversation. The first man said: "What a fine stick of timber that tree would make." The boy answered: "Good morning, Mr. Carpenter." The second man said: "That is fine bark." The boy answered: "Good morning, Mr. Tanner." The third man said: "I'll bet there's squirrels in that tree." The boy answered: "Good morning, Mr. Hunter." Each and every one of the men saw the tree in the light of his personal Apperception or Associated Interest.

Psychologists designate by the term "the apperceptive mass" the accumulated previous experiences, prejudices, temperament, inclination and desires which serve to modify the new perception or idea. The "apperceptive mass" is really the "character" or "human nature" of the individual. It necessarily differs in each individual, by *reason of the great variety of experiences, temperament, education, etc., among individuals. Upon a man's "apperceptive mass," or character, depends the nature and degree of his interest, and the objects which serve to inspire and excite it.*

It follows then that in order to arouse, induce and hold this Associated Interest of the prospect, the Salesman must present things, ideas or suggestions which will appeal directly to the imagination and feelings of the man before him, and which are associated with his desires, thoughts and habits. If we may be pardoned for the circular definition we would say that one's Associated Interest is aroused only by interesting things; and that the interesting things are those things which concern his interests. A man's interests always interest him—and his interests are usually those things which concern his advantage, success, personal well-being—in short his pocketbook, social position, hobbies, tastes, and satisfaction of his desires. Therefore the Salesman who can throw the mental spot-light on these interesting things, may secure and hold one's Associated Interest. Hence the psychology of the repeated statement: "I can save you money;" "I can increase your sales;" "I can reduce your expenses;" "I have something very choice;" or "I can give you a special advantage," etc.

*It may as well be conceded that business interest is selfish interest, and not altruistic. In order to interest a man in a business proposition he must be shown how it will benefit him in some way. He is not running a philanthropic institution, or a Salesman's Relief Fund, nor is he in business for his health—he is there to make money, and in order to interest him you must show him something to his advantage. And the first appeal of Associated Interest is to his feeling of Self Interest. It must be in the nature of the mention of "rats!" to a terrier, or "candy!" to a child. It must awaken pleasant associations in his mind, and pleasing images in his memory. If this effect is produced, he can be speedily moved to the succeeding phases of Imagination and Inclination. As Halleck says: "All feeling tends to excite desire. * * * A representative image of the thing desired is the necessary antecedent to* desire. If the child had never seen or heard of peaches he would have no desire for them." And, following this same figure, we may say that if the child has a taste for peaches he will be interested in the idea of peaches. And so when you say "peaches!" to him you have his Associated Interest, which will result in a mental image of the fruit followed by a desire to possess it, and he will listen to your talk regarding the subject of "peaches."

The following are the general psychological rules regarding Associated Interests:

I. Associated Interest attaches only to interesting things—that is to things associated with one's general desires and ideas.

II. Associated Interest will decline in force and effect unless some new attributes or features are presented—it requires variety in presentation of its object.

Macbain says: "One of the old time salesmen who used to sell the trade in the Middle West, beginning some thirty years ago, and following that vocation for several decades, used as his motto, 'I am here to do you good.' He did not make his statement general, either, in telling his customers how he could do it. He got right down to the vital affairs which touched his customers. He demonstrated it to them, and this personal demonstration is the kind that makes the sales."

Remember, always, that the phase of Associated Interest in a purchase is not the same as the phase of Demonstration and Proof. It is the "warming up" process, preceding the actual selling talk. It is the stage of "thawing out" the prospect and melting the icy covering of prejudice, caution and reluctance which encases him. Warm up your prospect by general statements of Associated Interest, and blow the coals by positive, brief, pointed confident statements of the good things you have in store for him. And, finally, remember that the sole purpose of your efforts at this state is to arouse in him the mental state of INTERESTED EXPECTANT ATTENTION! Keep blowing away at this spark until you obtain the blaze of Imagination and the heat of Desire.

V. Consideration. This mental state is defined as: "An examination, inquiry, or investigation into anything." It is the stage following Curiosity and Associated Interest, and tends toward an inquiry into the thing which has excited these feelings. Consideration, of course, must be preceded and accompanied by Interest. It calls for the phase of Attention excited by feeling, but a degree of voluntary attention is also manifested therewith. It is the "I think I will look into this matter" stage of the mental process of purchase. It is usually evidenced by a disposition to ask questions regarding the proposition, and to "see what there is to it, anyway." In Salesmanship, this stage of Consideration marks the passing from the stage of Approach on the Salesman's part, to that of the Demonstration. It marks the passage from Passive Interest to Active Interest—from the stage of being "merely interested" in a thing, to that of "interested investigation." Here is where the real selling work of the salesman begins. Here is where he begins to describe his proposition in detail, laying stress upon its desirable points. In the case of an advertisement, or a window display, the mental operation goes on in the buyer's mind in the same way, but without the assistance of the salesman. The "selling talk" of the advertisement must be stated or suggested by its text. If the Consideration is favorable and reveals sufficiently strong attractive qualities in the proposition or article, the mind of the buyer passes on to the next stage of the process which is known as:

VI. Imagination. This mental state is defined as: "The exercise of that power or faculty of the mind by which it conceives and forms ideal pictures of things communicated to it by the organs of sense." In the mental process of a purchase, the faculty of imagination takes up the idea of the object in which the Associated Interest has been aroused, and which has been made the subject of Consideration, and endeavors to picture the object in use and being employed in different ways, or as in possession of the buyer. One must use his imagination in order to realize what good a thing will be to him; how he may use it; how it will look; how it will sell; how it will serve its purpose; how it will "work out" or "make good" when purchased. A woman gazing at a hat will use her imagination to picture how she will look in it. The man looking at the book will use his imagination in picturing its uses and the pleasure to be derived therefrom. The business man will use his imagination to picture the probable sale of the goods, their display, their adaptability to his trade, etc. Another will picture himself enjoying the gains from his purchase. Imagination plays an important part in the psychology of the sale. It is the direct inciter of desire and inclination. The successful salesman realizes this, and feeds the flame of the imagination with the oil of Suggestion. In fact, Suggestion receives its power through the Imagination. The Imagination is the channel through which Suggestion reaches the mind. Salesmen and ad writers strive to arouse the imagination of their prospective customers by clever word-painting. The Imagination is the "direct wire" to Desire. From Imagination it is a short step to the next mental stage which is called:

VII. Inclination. This mental state is defined as: "A leaning or bent of the mind or will; desire; propensity." It is the "want to" feeling. It is the mental state of which Desire is an advanced stage. Inclination has many degrees. From a faint inclination or bent in a certain direction, it rises in the scale until it becomes an imperious demand, brooking no obstacle or hindrance. Many terms are employed to designate the various stages of Inclination, as for instance: Desire, wish, want, need, inclination, leaning, bent, predilection, propensity, penchant, liking, love, fondness, relish, longing, hankering, aspiration, ambition, appetite, hunger, passion, craving, lust, etc.

Desire is a strange mental quality, and one very difficult to define strictly. It is linked with feeling on one side, and with will on the other. Feeling rises to desire, and desire rises to the phase of will and endeavors to express itself in action. Halleck says of Desire: "It has for its object something which will bring pleasure or get rid of pain, immediate or remote, for the individual or for some one in whom he is interested. Aversion, or a striving to get away from something, is merely the negative aspect of desire." Inclination in its various stages is *aroused through the appeals to the feelings through the imagination. The feelings related to the several faculties are excited into action by a direct appeal to them through the imagination, and inclination or desired results. Appeal to Acquisitiveness will result in a feeling which will rise to inclination and desire for gain. Appeal to Approbativeness will act likewise in its own field. And so on through the list, each well-developed faculty being excited to feeling by the appropriate appeal through the imagination, and thus giving rise to Inclination which in turn strives to express itself in action through the will.*

In short, every man is a bundle of general desires, the nature and extent of which are indicated by his several faculties, and which result from heredity, environment, training, experience, etc. These desires may be excited toward a definite object by the proper emotional appeal through the imagination, and by suggestion. Desire must be created or aroused before action can be had, or the will manifest in action. For, at the last, we do things only because we "want to," directly or indirectly. Therefore, the important aim of the Salesman is to make his prospect "want to." And in order to make him "want to" he must make him see that his proposition is calculated to "bring pleasure, or get rid of pain, immediate or remote, for the individual or for someone else in whom he is interested." In business, the words "profit and loss" may be substituted for "pleasure and pain," although really, they are but forms of the latter. But even when the prospect is brought to the stage of strong inclination or desire, he does not always move to gratify the same. Why is this? What other mental process interferes? Let us see as we pass on to the next stage of the purchase, known as:

VIII. Deliberation. This mental state is defined as: "The act of deliberating and weighing facts and arguments in the mind, calmly and carefully." Here is manifested the action of thought and reason—the mental process of weighing and balancing facts, feelings, and inclinations. For it is not only facts and proofs which are weighed in the mental balance, but also feelings, desires, and fears. Pure logical reasoning inclines to strict logical processes based upon irrefragible facts, it is true—but there is but little pure logical reasoning. The majority of people are governed more by their feelings and inclinations—their loves and their fears—than by logic. It has been said: "People seek not reasons, but excuses for following their feelings." The real deliberation, in the majority of cases, is the weighing of probable advantages and disadvantages—of various likes and dislikes—of hopes and fears.

It is said that our minds are controlled by motives—and the strongest motive wins. We often find that when we think we desire a thing ardently, we then find that we also like something else better, or perhaps fear something else more than we desire the first thing. In such case, the strongest or most pressing feeling wins the day. The faculties here exert their different influences. Caution opposes Acquisitiveness. Acquisitiveness opposes Conscientiousness. Fear opposes Firmness. And so on. The deliberation is not only the weighing of facts, but also the weighing of feelings.

The process of Deliberation—the weighing of desires—the play and counterplay of motives—is well illustrated by a scene in a classical French comedy. "Jeppe," one of the characters, has been given money by his wife to buy her a cake of soap. He prefers to buy a drink with the coin, for his inclinations tend in that direction. But he knows that his wife will beat him if he so squanders the money. He deliberates over the pleasure to be derived from the drink, and the pain which would arise from the beating. "My stomach says drink—my back says soap," says Jeppe. He deliberates further. Then: "My stomach says Yes! My back says No!" cries the poor wight. The conflict between back and stomach rages still more fiercely. Then comes the deciding point: "Is not my stomach more to me than my back? Sure, it is! I say Yes!" cries Jeppe. And away to the tavern he marches. It has been remarked that if the active suggestion of the distant sight of his wife armed with the cudgel, had been added to the situation, Jeppe would have bought the soap. Or, if the tavern had not been so handy, the result might have been different. Sometimes a mental straw tips the scale. The above illustration contains the entire philosophy of the action of the mind in the process of Deliberation. The salesman will do well to remember it.

Halleck thus well states the immediate and remote factors in choice: "The immediate factors are * * * (1) a preceding process of desire; (2) the presence in consciousness of more than one represented object or end, to offer an alternative course of action; (3) deliberation concerning the respective merits of these objects; (4) the voluntary fiat of decision, which seems to embody most the very essence of will. The remote factors are extremely difficult to select. The sum total of the man is felt more in choice than anywhere else. * * * Before a second person could approximate the outcome, he would have to know certain remote factors, the principal being: (1) heredity; (2) environment; (3) education; (4) individual peculiarities." This eminent authority might well have added an additional element—a most important one—as follows: (5) SUGGESTION.

The Salesman watching carefully the shifting scale of Deliberation, injects a telling argument or suggestion into the scale, which gives weight to his side at a critical stage. He does this in many ways. He may neutralize an objection by a counter-fact. He adds another proof or fact here—a little more desire and feeling there, until he brings down the scale to a decision. It must be remembered that this Deliberation is not regarding the desirability of the proposition—the prospect has admitted his desire, either directly or indirectly, and is now engaged in trying to justify his desire by reason and expediency. He is seeking for reasons or "excuses" to back up his desire, or perhaps, is endeavoring to strike a balance of his conflicting desires and feelings. His mental debate is not over the question of desiring the goods, but over the expediency and probable result of buying them. It is the "to buy or not to buy" stage. This is a delicate part of the process of the purchase, and many prospects act like "see-saws" during the process. The clever Salesman must be ready with the right argument at the right place. To him this is the Argumentive Stage. Finally, if the Salesman's efforts are successful, the balance drops, and the process passes to the next stage, known as—

IX. Decision. This mental stage is defined as: "The mental act of deciding, determining, or settling any point, question, difference, or contest." It is the act of the will, settling the dispute between the warring faculties, feelings, ideas, desires and fears. It is will acting upon reason, or (alas! too often, upon mere feeling). Without entering into a metaphysical discussion, let us remind you that the practical psychology of the day holds that "the strongest motive at the moment wins the choice." This strongest motive may be of reason or of feeling; conscious or unconscious; but strongest at that moment it must be, or it would not win. And this strongest motive is strongest merely because of our character or "nature" as manifested at that particular moment, in that particular environment, under the particular circumstances, and subject to the particular suggestions. The choice depends more upon association than we generally realize, and association is awakened by suggestion. As Halleck says: "It is not the business of the psychologist to state what power the association of ideas ought to have. It is for him to ascertain what power it does have." And as Ziehen says: "We cannot think as we will, but we must think just as those associations which happen to be present prescribe." This being the case, the Salesman must realize that the Decision is based always upon (1) the mental states of the man at that moment; plus (2) the added motives supplied by the Salesman. It is "up to" the Salesman to supply those motives, whether they be facts, proofs, appeals to reason, or excitement of feeling. Hope, fear, like, dislike—these are the potent motives in most cases. In business, these things are known as "profit or loss." All the faculties of the mind supply motives which aroused may be thrown into the balance affecting decision. This is what argument, demonstration and appeal seek to do—supply motives.

(Note:—It might naturally be supposed that when the final stage of Decision has been reached, the mental process of purchase is at an end. But, not so. Will has three phases: Desire, Decision, and Action. We have passed through the first two, but Action still is unperformed. A familiar example is that of the man in bed in the morning. He ponders *over the question of rising, and finally decides to get up. But action does not necessarily result. The trigger of Action has not been pulled, and the spring released. So thus we have another mental state, known as:—)*

*X. Action. This mental state is defined as: "Volition carried into effect." Mill says: "Now what is an action? Not one, but a series of two things: the state of mind called a volition, followed by an effect. The volition or intention to produce the effect is one thing; the effect produced in consequence of the intention is another thing; the two together constitute the action." Halleck says: "For a completed act of will, there must be action along the line of the decision. Many a decision has not aroused the motor centers to action, nor quickened the attention, for any length of time. There are persons who can frame a dozen decisions in the course of a morning, and never carry out one of them. Sitting in a comfortable chair, it may take one but a very short time to form a decision that will require months of hard work. * * * Some persons can never seem to understand that resolving to do a thing is not the same as doing it. * * * There may be desire, deliberation, and decision; but if these do not result in action along the indicated line, the process of will is practically incomplete." Many a person decides to do a thing but lacks the something necessary to release the motive impulses. They tend to procrastinate, and delay the final act. These people are sources of great care and work to the Salesman. Some men can get their prospects to the deciding point, but fail to get them to act. Others seem specially adapted to "closing" these cases. It requires a peculiar knack to "close"—the effort is entirely psychological. We shall consider it in a subsequent chapter under the head of "Closing." To be a good "closer" is the ambition of every Salesman, for it is the best paid branch of his profession. It depends largely upon the scientific application of suggestion. To lead a prospect to Action, is to pull the trigger of his will. To this end all the previous work has been directed. Its psychology is subtle. What makes you finally get out of bed in the morning, after having "decided to" several times without resulting* *action? To understand this, is to understand the process of the final Action in the mind of the buyer. Is it not worth learning?*

In the succeeding chapters we shall consider the several stages of the "Salesman's Progress" toward a sale—the Approach, the Demonstration, and the Closing. In these stages of the Salesman, we shall see the action and reaction upon the Mind of the Buyer, along the lines of the Psychology of the Purchase. In the Sale-Purchase the minds of the Salesman and the Buyer meet. The result is the Signed Order. The psychological process of the Sale is akin to the progress of a game of chess or checkers. And neither is the result of chance—well defined principles underlie each, and established methods are laid down for the student.

What I love about this section is how the sale can be broken down into a process of how a buyer is going to make a decision. And when you are able to craft your sales pitch or presentation to match the process the buyer's mind will go through to make a purchase, you can increase your close rate by a lot. Following what is comfortable to a buyer is profitable.

One thing to pay particular attention to is what gets a buyer to talk to you. Many years ago, my sister was talking to a prospect about buying office equipment. She told me she was nervous about the meeting. I told her if she had a meeting with the president of the company then he needed something and is hoping she has it so he can move on to something else.

People are busy. I think what can throw salespeople off is when they are able to spark curiosity with their pitch but find a lot of their conversations don't end up with a closed deal. Having an understanding of what makes someone buy is powerful. You won't get discouraged as much. When you can recognize what is happening in the sales process you can stay on point.

CHAPTER TWELVE

Secret 10
The Approach
- William Walker Atkinson

Old salesmen hold that in the psychology of the sale there is no more important stage or phase than the introductory stage—the stage of the Approach. Pierce says: "Experienced salesmen will tell you that the first five minutes in front of a prospect is worth more than all the remainder in the matter of getting the check. Why? Because it is then that the prospect is forming his impressions of you. Usually he is obliged to form this quick size-up of the man he meets, in order to conserve his time for important duties. Therefore it is your duty to have this first impression the best within your power. And the best way to develop this is to be genuine." But it must never be lost sight of that the First Impression is solely for the purpose of obtaining an entrance for the fine edge of your wedge of salesmanship, which you must then proceed to drive home to its logical conclusion,—the Order. An impression for impression's sake is a fallacy. Remember the old story of the Salesman who wrote in that he was not making sales, but that he was "making a good impression on my customers." The firm wired back to him: "Go out and make some more impressions—on a snow bank." Do not lose sight of the real object of your work, in obtaining the preliminary results.

The National Cash Register Company instructs its salesmen regarding the First Impression, as follows: "Remember, the first five minutes of speaking to a man is likely to make or break you as far as that sale is concerned. If you are in any way antagonistic or offensive to him, you have hurt your chances badly from the start. If you have failed to definitely please or attract him, you have not done enough. It isn't sufficient to be merely a negative quantity. You should make a positive favorable impression, and not by cajolery nor attempted wit nor cleverness. The only right way to gain a man's liking is to deserve it. The majority of men do not often know just what the characteristics of a man are which makes him pleasing or displeasing to them; but they feel pleased or displeased, attracted or repulsed, or indifferent, and the feeling is definite and pronounced, even though they cannot understand just what makes it. A storekeeper in the smallest way of business in a little country village is just as susceptible of being pleased or offended as any merchant prince. It should never be forgotten that whatever his position may be, 'a man's a man for a' that.'"

It is not so much what a man says when he approaches the prospect, as the way he acts. It is his manner, rather than his speech. And back of his manner is his Mental Attitude. Without going into subtle psychological theorizing, we may say that it may be accepted as a working hypotheses that a man radiates his Mental State, and that those he approaches feel these radiations. It may be the suggestion of manner, or it may be something more subtle—no use discussing theories here, we haven't the time—the fact is that it acts as radiations would act. This being recognized it will be seen that the man's Mental Attitude in the Approach must be right. In the previous chapters we have had much to say to you regarding the factors which go to create the Mental Attitude. Now is the time to manifest what you have learned and practice—for you are making the Approach.

Carry in mind Holman's catechism, of which we have told you. Maintain your Self-Respect, and remember that you are a MAN. Pierce says of this: "One reason for this is that self-respect is necessary in your work. And self-respect cannot obtain where there is lack of confidence either in your own ability or in your line of goods. Assuming that you take only such a line as you yourself can enthusiastically endorse, it must be remembered that your goods place you absolutely on a par with the merchant. Hence, you talk to him shoulder to shoulder, as it were. You are not as a slave to a master! as a hireling to a lord; as a worm to a mountain; although this is the usual attitude untrained salesmen consciously or unconsciously assume. They are timid. They feel they might know their goods better. They feel, perhaps, that the prospect knows their goods or their competitors' goods better than they do themselves. Fear is written all over their faces as the approach is made. Nine-tenths of the fear is due to ignorance of the goods. The other tenth is lack of experience."

Regarding this matter of Fear, we would say that the experience of the majority of men who have lived active and strenuous lives, meeting with all sorts of people under all sorts of circumstances, is that the cause of Fear of people and things exists chiefly in the imagination. It is the fear of anticipation rather than the fear of actual conditions. It is like the fear felt upon approaching a dentist's office—worse than the actual experience of the chair. Suspense and fearful expectation are two of the great sources of human weakness. Experience shows us that the majority of things we fear never happen; that those which do happen are never so bad as we had feared. Moreover, experience teaches us that when a real difficulty confronts us, we usually are given the strength and courage to meet and bear it, or to overcome it—while in our moments of fearful anticipation these helpful factors are not apparent.[Pg 172] Sufficient for the moment are the evils thereof—it is not the troubles of the moment which bear us down, but the burdens of future moments which we have added to our load. The rule is to meet each question or obstacle as it arises, and not to add fear of trouble beyond to the work of the moment. Do not cross your bridge till you come to it. The majority of feared things melt away when you come up to them—they partake of the nature of the mirage. It is the ghosts of things which never materialize which cause us the greatest fear. Banish Fearthought from your Mental Attitude when you make the Approach.

But, a word of warning here: Do not become "fresh" or impudent because you feel Self Reliant and Fearless. While realizing that you are a Man, do not forget that the prospect is also one. Impudence is a mark of weakness rather than of strength—strong men are above this petty thing. Be polite and courteous. The true gentleman is both self-respecting and polite. And, after all is said and done, the best Approach that a Salesman can make is that of a GENTLEMAN. This will win in the long run, and the consciousness[Pg 173] of having so acted will tend to strengthen the Salesman and preserve his self-respect. Remember not only to manifest the self-respect of a gentleman—but also to observe the obligations of politeness and courtesy which are incumbent upon a gentleman. Noblesse oblige—"nobility imposes obligations."

If you want a maxim of action and manner, take this one: "Act as a gentleman should." If you want a touchstone upon which to test manner and action, take this: "Is this the act of a gentleman?" If you will follow this advice you will acquire a manner which will be far superior to one based upon artificial rules or principles—a natural manner—because the manner of a gentleman is the expression of true and pure courtesy, and will be respected as such by all, whether they, themselves, observe it or not. We have seen many instances in which the maintenance of the true gentlemanly spirit under strong provocation has completely disarmed boorishness, and won friendship and regard from those apparently opposing it at the time.

The first psychological element of a Sale is that of the First Impression upon the buyer.[Pg 174] And the impression must be of a favorable kind. There must be nothing to create a bad impression for this will distract the attention from the purpose of the Approach to the particular object awakening the unpleasant impression. The first point preliminary to gaining attention, is to know the name of the man you are approaching; and if possible just where he is. Nothing is more demoralizing to the Salesman, and more likely to break up the psychological influence of the Approach, than a lack of knowledge of the name and identity of the man you wish to see. The miscarriage of an Approach occasioned by mistaking the person should be avoided. If you do not know your man, or where he is in the office, it will be well to inquire of the others present, politely of course, where "Mr. X's" desk is. If you happen to ask this question of "Mr. X" himself, you can easily adjust yourself to the occasion. The fiasco of approaching "Mr. A" and greeting him as "Mr. X" is apt to be confusing and weakening, and tends to bring the element of ridicule into the interview, unless the Salesman has the tact and wit to pass it off. If possible,[Pg 175] avoid asking for "the proprietor," or inquiring of a man, "are you the proprietor?" If you do not know the proprietor's name, ask it of some one.

The National Cash Register people say to their salesmen: "It is manifestly improper to describe a definite form of words and require salesmen to use them in all cases when they approach business men at the first interview. What would be proper to say to one man under given circumstances might be unsuitable to say to another under different circumstances. Much must be left to the discretion of the salesman. At the same time there are certain leading statements to be made, and certain ways of making them which experience has shown to be well adapted to the end in view. * * * It is not necessary that this introductory talk should be long. Often a short talk is more convincing. We do not advise salesmen to introduce themselves by sending in a card, but prefer that they should depend wholly on what they are able to say to secure a hearing. We strongly disapprove of obscure introductions and all tricks, and believe that a man[Pg 176] who has something worth saying, and is not ashamed of his business, can make known his errand in a bold, straightforward manner. A salesman should adapt himself to his man, but at the same time he should have a fixed idea of what he has to say. He should be dignified and earnest. * * * As soon as you do succeed in reaching the proprietor, and have said to him, 'Good morning! Is this Mr. Johnson?' then say directly and plainly, 'I represent the National Cash Register Company.' This immediately puts you on a square footing, and if he has anything to say against your business it will draw his fire immediately. If he has nothing to say, proceed to business at once, but don't under any circumstances say, 'I called to sell you a register,' or 'I called to tell you about our registers,' but put it rather in this way, 'I want to interest you in our methods for taking care of transactions with customers in your store.' The difference between the two ways of saying it is that one begins with your end of the business—the thing that interests you; while the other begins at his end of it—the thing presumably interesting to him."

We specially direct the student's attention to the above paragraph. It contains in a nutshell the whole philosophy of the introductory talk of the Approach. It is the essence of the experience and knowledge of the thousands of salesmen of the great selling organization of the large concern named, and is right to the point, and what is still more important, it is scientifically correct, and based upon true psychological principles.

The Salesman in making the Approach should not act as if he were in a hurry, nor should he dawdle. He should go about it in a business-like manner showing his realization of the value of time, and yet acting as if he had the time necessary for the transaction of that particular piece of business, just as he would if the buyer had called on him instead of vice versa. Don't swagger or strut, or act as if you were the proprietor. Act the part of the real business man who is at ease and yet is attending to business. Do not try to "rush" the customer in the Approach—you are calling on him and must appear to defer to him in the matter of opening the conversation, in a respectful and yet self-respecting manner. The better poised and balanced you are in manner, the more he will respect you, no matter how he may act. It is much easier for a buyer to turn down an ill-bred boorish caller than one who shows the signs of being a gentleman. In fact the boorish caller invites the turn-down—he suggests it by his manner; while the gentleman suggests respectful treatment. The line of least resistance in suggestion is the one most natural for people to follow.

Some salesmen try to grasp the hand of the customer at the beginning. This is all right if the customer be a jovial "hale fellow, well met" kind of a man, but if he be reserved and dignified he will be apt to resent your pushing this attention upon him. The thing to do is to make him feel like shaking hands—this is an important point, which counts if gained. You can generally tell from his manner and expression whether to extend your hand. You must trust to your intuitions in "sizing up" your man. What has been said regarding the mind of the buyer will help you, and what data you have collected will also be of use, but at the last you must depend upon your own intuition to a considerable extent. Experience develops this intuitive faculty. Some salesmen thrust their cards into the hands of a prospect when they introduce themselves. This is poor psychology, for it serves to attract the prospect's attention to the card and away from the salesman. Introduce yourself verbally, simply and distinctly, and then get down to business.

If you see a man is busy with someone else, or with something in particular—wait for him. Don't break into his occupation, until he looks up and gives you the psychological signal to proceed. Never interrupt another salesman who may be talking to the prospect. This is not only a point in fair play and business courtesy, but is very good business policy in addition. When you begin your introductory talk, get right to the point, and don't beat around the bush as so many do. Get down to business—get over the agony of suspense—take the plunge. Remember always, that to the prospect your little story is not as stale or stereotyped as it may be to you—so put earnestness into it, and tell it just as if you were relating it for the first time to someone who had requested it from you. Maintain your interest, if you would arouse that of the prospect.

Never commit the folly of asking a prospect: "Are you busy?" or, "I fear you are busy, sir?" This is a very bad suggestion for the prospect, and makes it easy for him to say "Yes!" You mould bullets for him to *fire at you. If he really is too busy to give you the proper attention, you may do well to tell him so, and then get out—but never suggest anything of this kind to him if you expect to proceed. It is akin to the doleful "You don't want to buy any matches, sir, do you?" of the forlorn vendors of small articles who float into offices at times. Never make it easy for a prospect to turn you down—or out. If he is going to do these things, make him work hard to do it. This might seem like needless advice, but many young salesmen commit this particular fault. Avoid the apologetic attitude and manner—you have nothing to apologize for. You are using up your time as much as the prospect's time—let it go at that. Never apologize for anything but a fault or mistake. Your call is not a fault or a mistake—unless you make it so by assuming it to be such. Some men would like to apologize for being alive, but they never make salesmen. Be careful what adverse suggestions you may put into the prospect's mind by this apologizing and "explaining" business. What's the use of this nonsense anyway—it never sold any goods, and never will. It is merely a sign of weakness and lack of nerve. Better stop it.*

The trouble with these apologetic and explanatory fellows is that they do not thoroughly believe in the merit of their propositions. If they really believed as they should—if they had "sold themselves"—they would realize that the prospect needs their goods, and, that although he might not know it now, he is being done a favor by having his attention called to them. A Salesman has no need to apologize to a customer, unless he has need to apologize to himself—and if he is not right on the latter score he had better change his line and get something to sell that he is not ashamed of, or get out of the business altogether. No man ever feels ashamed of anything in which he thoroughly believes and appreciates.

The following advice from the National Cash Register people, is like everything else they say, very good: "Do not attempt to talk to a man who is not listening, who is writing a letter or occupying himself in any other way while you are talking. That's useless, and is a loss of self-respect and of his respect. If he cannot give you his attention, say to him: 'I see that you are busy. If you can give me your attention for a few minutes I shall be pleased; but I don't want to interrupt you, if you cannot spare the time, and I will call again.' Try to understand and feel thoroughly the distinction between confidence and familiarity. Never fail in respect either to yourself or to the man with whom you are talking. Never be familiar with him. Never put your hand on his shoulder or on his arm, nor take hold of his coat. Such things are repugnant to a gentleman—and you should assume that he is one. Never pound the desk or shake your finger at a prospect. Don't shout at him as if sound would take the place of sense. Don't advance at him and talk so excitedly under his nose that he will back away from you for fear of being run over, as if you were a trolley-car. I have seen a sales agent back a prospect half way across a room in this way. Don't compel a man to listen to you by loud or fast talking. Don't make him feel that he can't get a word in edgewise and has to listen until you are out of breath. This is not the sort of compulsion to make customers. But make him believe that you have something to say and will say it quickly. Put yourself in his place from the very start. Make him feel, not that you are trying to force your business upon him, but that you want to discuss how his business may be benefited by you."

One of the best salesmen this particular company ever had has passed down to the selling corps of that concern the following axiom: "If you do but one thing, in approaching a prospect, say, 'It will save you money,' seven times, and you have made a good Approach." And so say we. Concrete facts, stated in terse terms, are the essence of the opening talk and the life of the Approach.

What we have said so far has reference to the stage of First Impression, which followed the preliminary stage of Involuntary Attention which was caused by your presence. The purpose of the favorable First Impression is to make the way easy for the real process of selling which is to follow. The principle of First Impression rests upon the associated experience of the buyer, and its effect arises from suggestion. The hasty, general idea or impression of the Salesman's *personality, which we call the First Impression, is almost unconscious on the part of the prospect, and is due largely to the suggestion of association. That is, the prospect has met other people manifesting certain characteristics, and has fallen into the habit of hasty generalization, or classification of people in accordance with certain traits of appearance, manner, etc. This is the operation of the psychological principle of the Association of Ideas, and may be influenced by what is known as the Suggestion of Association. The following quotation from the volume of this series entitled "Suggestion and Auto-Suggestion," will make clearer this principle:*

"*This form of Suggestion is one of the most common phases. It is found on all sides, and at all times. The mental law of association makes it very easy for us to associate certain things with certain other things, and we will find that when one of the things is recalled it will bring with it its associated impression. * * * We are apt to associate a well-dressed man, of commanding carriage, travelling in an expensive automobile, with the idea of wealth and influence. And, accordingly, when some adventurer of the 'J. Rufus Wallingford' type travels our way, clad in sumptuous apparel, with the air of an Astorbilt, and a $10,000 (hired) automobile, we hasten to place our money and valuables in his keeping, and esteem ourselves honored by having been accorded the privilege.*"

The Suggestion of Authority also plays its part in the First Impression, and in all the stages of sale in fact. This form of suggestion is described in the book just mentioned, as follows: "*Let some person posing as an authority, or occupying a position of command, calmly state a fallacy with an air of wisdom and conviction, without any 'ifs' or 'buts,' and many otherwise careful people will accept the suggestion without question; and, unless they are afterward forced to analyze it by the light of reason they will let this seed find lodgement in their minds, to blossom and bear fruit thereafter. The explanation is that in such cases the person suspends the critical attention which is usually interposed by the attentive will, and allows the idea to enter his mental castle unchallenged, and to influence other ideas in the future. It is like* a man assuming a lordly air and marching past the watchman at the gate of the mental fortress, where the ordinary visitor is challenged and severely scrutinized; his credentials examined; and the mark of approval placed upon him before he may enter. * * * The acceptance of such suggestions is akin to a person bolting a particle of food, instead of masticating it. As a rule we bolt many a bit of mental provender, owing to its stamp of real or pretended authority. And many persons understanding this phase of suggestion take advantage of it, and 'use it in their business' accordingly. The confidence-man, as well as the shrewd politician and the seller of neatly printed gold-mines, imposes himself upon the public by means of an air of authority, or by what is known in the parlance of the busy streets as 'putting up a good front.' Some men are all 'front,' and have nothing behind their authoritative air—but that authoritative air provides them with a living."

The suggestion of associated manner, appearance and air—the "good front," in fact—is the principal element in the favorable First Impression. The balance is a mixture of tact, diplomacy, common sense, and intuition. But remember this always: the best "front" is the real one—the one which is the reflection of the right Mental Attitude and Character—the "front" of the Gentleman. If you lack this, the nearer you can act it out, the better for yourself. But no imitation is as good as the genuine article. The true Gentleman is the scientific mixture of strength and courtesy—the manifestation of "the iron hand in the velvet glove." So much for the First Impression.

The mental stages of Curiosity and Associated Interest on the part of the buyer are also to be induced by the Salesman in the Approach. We have described these phases in the chapter entitled "The Psychology of the Purchase," this particular part of which should be re-read at this point. A few additional words on these points, however, will not be out of place here.

Regarding the phase of Curiosity, we would say that it will be well if you can manage the opening talk to the prospect so as to "keep him guessing a little," while still holding his Associated Interest. Curiosity whets a man's interest just as Worcestershire sauce whets his appetite. The key to the arousing of Curiosity is the idea of "something new;" a new idea; a new pattern, a new device, etc. The mind of the average man likes "something new"—even the old fogy likes something new in his old favorites, new bottles for his good old wine. The idea of newness and novelty tends to arouse a man's inquisitiveness and imagination. And if you can start these faculties working you have done well, for Associated Interest is closely allied thereto. When you get a prospect to the stage of asking questions, either verbally or mentally, you have the game well started.

Never make the mistake of asking the man if he "wants to buy so-and-so." Of course he doesn't at that stage, particularly if you ask him in that way. It is too easy for him to say No! It is almost as bad as that stock illustration of adverse suggestion: "You don't want to buy any so-and-so, do you mister?" which brings a ready "No!" from the average person. Nor do you want to say: "I have called to see if I cannot sell you so-and-so, to-day, Mr. X." Or, "Can I sell you some so-and-so, this morning, Mr. Z?" This form of arousing interest is based on erroneous psychological principles. Of course, the prospect doesn't want to buy or be sold at this stage of the game—the sale is the finishing stage. This plan is like cutting a log of wood with the butt-end of the axe—you are presenting the wrong end of the proposition. You can never arouse Curiosity or Associated Interest in this way. Forget the words "You buy" and "I sell" for the moment—in fact the less you use them at any stage the better it will be, for they are too unpleasantly suggestive of the opening of pocket-books to be agreeable to the prospect. There are excellent substitutes for these terms—terms which suggest profit, advantage, saving and pleasure to the mind of the buyer, rather than ideas of expenditure and "giving up." Try to suggest the incoming stream of money to your buyer—not the outgoing one. The reason is obvious, if you understand the laws of suggestion and psychology.

In short, let your appeal at this stage be entirely to the Self Interest, Pleasure, and Curiosity of the prospect. Try to get him warmed up, and his imagination working. *If you can do this he will forget his other objects of attention, and will lay aside his armor of suggestive defence and his shield of instinctive resistance to one whom he thinks "wants to sell something" and open his pocket-book. This is the stage in which you must get in the sharp end of your psychological wedge. Here is where you need the keen edge of your axe—the butt-end may be reserved for the Decision and Closing.*

As far as possible, do not ask questions to which the prospect can answer "No!" at this stage. Fence him off on this point, and dodge every sign of a forthcoming negative. But if he does get out a "No!" or two—do not hear him. Let his "No!" slip off like water from a duck's back—refuse to admit it to your consciousness—deny it mentally—refuse the evidence of your ears. This is no time for "Noes"—go right ahead, unconscious of the words. Keep on appealing to his Interest, in the phases of Curiosity and Associated Interest. Your aim here is to get the prospect to the stage of Consideration. This stage is indicated by his asking a question showing a desire to know the particulars of your proposition. The question may show but a shade of interest, but it marks a move in the game. It is the prospect's answering move to your opening. It is an important psychological moment in the game. The next move is yours!

And that move is on the plane of the Demonstration—for the stage of the approach has now been passed.

Before passing on to the consideration of the stage of Demonstration, we desire to call your attention to the following excellent advice regarding the matter of rebuffs which are so often met with in the stage of Approach. It is from the pen of W.C. Holman, and appeared in his magazine "Salesmanship." Mr. Holman says: "A crack-a-jack salesman will receive a rebuff as gracefully and easily and with as little damage to himself as a professional baseball player will take in a red-hot liner that a batter drives at him, and go right on playing the game as if nothing had happened. An amateur salesman will want to quit playing, *or call the attention of the umpire to the malicious intent of the batter. A blow that would knock the ordinary man off his pins will do nothing more than to give a professional boxer a chance to show his agility and win applause. If you drop a plank on a cork in the water with a tremendous splash the cork will bob up as serenely as if nothing had happened, and lie quietly once more on the unruffled surface of the water. And so a clever salesman, when a smashing blow is aimed at him by a surly prospect, will merely sidestep gracefully and continue calmly with the prosecution of his purpose. * * * Self-control disarms all ill natured attacks."*

The approach here is face to face. Many points work for phone sales as well. It's not a coincidence that when he discusses the timid salesperson he points out that they haven't sold themselves on what they are selling. They don't believe in what they are selling so they don't believe they can sell it. If you aren't sold your prospect won't be either. Sell yourself first.

I love that he says you shouldn't try to talk to someone who's not listening and how you have to be careful of the words you choose so you don't lose the prospect's interest in talking to you. These may seem like obvious things, but a lot of sales calls I've listened to ended badly because the sales rep didn't have a clear idea of how they should approach the call.

Sales scripts are really great to use. Having a crafted intro, transitions, and closings scripted out make every presentation spot on. When a salesperson knows what they are saying, how they are saying it, where the call is going and how to keep the conversation on track, they close more deals. You have to have a process. You have to know what you're going to say on every call.

There are a lot of sales coaches, mentors and trainers who will tell their students not to use scripts and that they aren't good to use. Those people have never learned how to properly use a script. If they had, they would be teaching every single person they trained to master using scripts. I trained over 400 sales reps in how to use scripts. It's a game changer for the closer.

The discussion on establishing oneself as an authority when talking to a prospect is like knowing your product or service better than your prospect does. You have to do your homework when it comes to sales. You have to be prepared to be effective. You have to have answers. And even though this is so obvious, there are times when everyone fails at this on a call.

He mentions that in the approach your focus should be on the *Self Interest, Pleasure, and Curiosity of the prospect.* My mom sold real estate for 18 yrs after being a stay-at-home mom raising me and my brother and sister. She worked for a lady who told her agents, sales is about your customer. It's about them, not you. And it works. My mom got a lot of referrals and did well.

Staying focused on the goal, maintaining the course and not getting thrown off in the approach is easier said than done at times in sales. It's the professional salesperson who is able to adapt to the unexpected and bring a prospect around to talking to them. It takes practice like anything else. If you want to be good at sales, keep doing it. Don't give up. Stay in the game.

CHAPTER THIRTEEN

Secret 11
The Demonstration
- William Walker Atkinson

In the last chapter we left the Salesman at that stage of the Approach where the prospect manifests enough interest to ask a question or make an interrogative objection. This is an important psychological point or stage in the game, and here the Approach merges into the Demonstration on the part of the Salesman; and the stage of passive attention on the part of the prospect merges into that of active attention, discussion and Consideration. The moment that the prospect ceases to be a passive listener, and displays enough active interest to ask a question or make an interrogative objection, the great game of the sale is on in earnest. The Demonstration has begun.

This stage of the sale closely resembles a game of chess or checkers. The approach and preliminary talk of the Salesman is the first move in the game; the answer, question or objection of the prospect is the second move—then the real game or discussion is on. It is now "up to" the Salesman to make his second move, which is a reply move to that of the prospect. And this particular move is a highly important one in the great game of the sale. Like an important early move in checkers or chess the success or failure of the whole game may depend on it, so it is well to have this move mapped out as a part of your preliminary study.

Macbain truthfully says of the first remark of the prospect: "The customer is not going to commit himself in response to the first remark. He always holds considerable in reserve. An objection—either expressed or implied—can always be counted on. It may vary from a general 'busy' statement, or 'no interest in what is about to be submitted,' or it may be a specific statement—even heated, in fact—that the one approached has 'no time for the salesman or his house.'"

But, just as in chess or checkers there are certain "replies" indicated for every one of the first few opening moves, all of which are fully stated and explained in text books on these games, so in the great game of Salesmanship there are certain replies indicated for these preliminary moves on the part of the prospect. The large selling concerns have schools of instruction, personal or correspondence, in which the Salesman is furnished with the appropriate and logical answers to the objections and questions usually advanced by the prospect. It will be found that there are really but few moves of this kind in the game of the average prospects—they tend to say the same things under the same circumstances, and there is always an appropriate answer. The salesman will acquire many of these answers by experience, conversation with older salesmen, or by instruction from his salesmanager or the house. Each line has its own stock of objections, and its own stock of replies thereto.

There are two general classes of replies to objections, which apply to nearly every kind of proposition. The first is that of deftly catching the objection on your mental fencing-foil, allowing it to glance off, and at the same time getting a thrust on your opponent. President Patterson of the National Cash Register Company is credited with special cleverness in this kind of reply, and his salesmen are said to be instructed to listen carefully to the prospect's objection and then to turn it back on him by a remark based on the principle of: "Why, that's the very reason why you should," etc. In other words the objection should *be twisted into an argument in favor of the proposition. In the hands of a master this form of reply is very effective, and often brings results by reason of its daring and unexpectedness. But it is not every one who has the skill to use it to advantage.*

The second class of reply is based upon what is called indirect Resistance, which, by the way, is often the strongest form of resistance, and accomplishes its intended effect while avoiding the opposition and antagonism of Direct Resistance. Some writers on the subject have called this "Non-Resistance," obviously a misnomer for it is a form of resistance although subtly disguised. It is analogous to the tree that bends in order to avoid breaking under the blasts of the storm; of the flexible steel which bends to the pressure, instead of breaking as would iron; but both of which spring back into place immediately. It is generally very poor policy to directly oppose the prospect upon minor points—the main point is what you are after. And the main point is the order—the rest is immaterial and unimportant. Let us contrast Direct-Resistance and Indirect-Resistance, and see the points of each.

In Direct Resistance the minor objections of the prospect are met with the answer: "You are wrong there, Mr. X;" or, "You are entirely mistaken;" or, "You take the wrong view;" or, as we heard in one instance: "Your objection is ridiculous." The Direct Resistance is necessary in a few contingencies, or upon rare occasions, but it should be sparingly and cautiously used. It is a desperate remedy indicated only for desperate diseases. The Indirect Resistance expresses itself in answers of: "That is possibly true in some cases, but," etc.; or, "There is much truth in what you say, Mr. X, but," etc.; or, "As a general proposition that is probably correct, but," etc.; or, "I quite agree with you, Mr. X. that (etc.) but in this particular case I think an exception should be made," etc. The value of this form of resistance lies in the fact that it costs you nothing to allow the prospect to retain his own ideas and entertain his own prejudices, provided they do not interfere with the logic of your general argument, nor affect your main point, the order.

You are not a missionary or a pedagogue—you are just a Salesman and your business is to take orders. Let the old fellow keep his foolish ideas and intolerant prejudices, providing you can steer him straight to the ordering point. The active principle in Indirect Resistance is to get rid of his general objections in the easiest and shortest way, by allowing him to retain them, and concentrating your and his attention and interest upon the particular points of your proposition—the positive and material points of your particular case. Avoid disputes on non-essentials, generalities, and immaterial points. You are not striving for first prize in debate—you're after orders. Remember the legal principles of the "pertinent, relevant, and material" points, and sidetrack the "immaterial, irrelevant and impertinent" side-issues, even if you have to tacitly admit them in Indirect Resistance. Here it is in a nutshell: Sidetrack and Sidestep the Non-Essentials.

The Salesman has now reached the point in which the prospect is manifesting the psychological stage of Consideration—the stage in which he is willing to "look into" the matter, or rather into the subject or object of the proposition. This stage must not be confused with that of Deliberation, in which the prospect weighs the pros and cons of whether he should purchase. The two stages are quite different. The present stage—that of Consideration—is merely the phase of examination, investigation or inquiry into the matter, to see if there is really anything of real practical interest in it for himself. It is more than mere Associated Interest, for it has passed into the manifestation of interested investigation. In many cases the process never gets beyond this stage, particularly if the Salesman does not understand the psychology of the process. Many salesmen make the mistake of trying to make their closing talk at this point—but this is a mistake. The prospect must understand something about the details of the proposition, or the qualities and characteristics of the goods, before he uses his imagination or feels inclination to possess the thing. So here is where the work of explanation comes in.

The term "Demonstration" has two general means, each of which is exemplified by stages in the Salesman's work of Demonstration. The first meaning, and stage, is: "A showing or pointing out; an indication, manifestation or exhibition." The second meaning, and stage, is: "The act of proving clearly, by incontrovertible proof and indubitable evidence, beyond the possibility of doubt or contradiction." The first stage is that of "showing and pointing out"—the second, that of of "proof." The first is that of presenting the features of a thing—the second, that of logical argument and proof. And, therefore, remember that you are now at the stage of "showing and pointing out," and not that of "argument and proof."

Regarding the matter of "showing and pointing out" the features and characteristics of your goods or proposition, you should always remember that the prospect does not know the details of your proposition or article of sale as you do—or as you should know. The subject is not "stale" to him, as it may have become to you if you have not kept up your enthusiasm. Therefore, while avoiding needless waste of time, do not make the mistake of rushing this point of the demonstration and thus neglecting the important features. Better one feature well explained and emphasized, than a score hurried over in a sloppy manner. It is better to concentrate upon a few leading and striking points of demonstration, of material interest to the prospect, and to assume that he does not know anything about them except as he may show his knowledge by questions or objections—all this in a courteous manner, of course, avoiding the "know it all" air. The prospect must have time to allow the points to sink into his mind—some men are slower than others in this respect. Watch the prospect's face to see by his expression whether or not he really understands what you are saying. Better present one point in a dozen ways, to obtain understanding, than to present a dozen points in one way and fail to be understood.

In order to demonstrate your goods or proposition at this stage, you must have fully acquainted yourself with them, and also have arranged the telling points in a natural and logical order of presentation, working from the simple up to the complex. Be careful not to suggest buying at this point, lest your prospect take fright and lose interest in the demonstration. He is naturally in a defensive mood, for he scents the appeal to his pocket book in the distance—you must try to take his mind off this point by arousing his interested attention in the details of your goods or proposition. Explain the details just as you would if the prospect had called upon you for the purpose of investigation. In fact, if you can work yourself up to the proper Mental Attitude you may effect the psychological change by which the positions may be reversed, and so that it will instinctively seem to the prospect that he is calling on you and not you on him. There is an important psychological point here which you would do well to remember. The man who is called upon always has "the move" on the caller—if you can reverse this psychological condition, you have gained a great advantage. An awakened personal interest in the details of a proposition, on the part of the prospect, tends to reverse the conditions.

If you would understand what a scientific demonstration of an article or proposition is like, it would pay you to listen to the demonstration by a well-trained salesman of the National Cash Register Company. This company drills its salesmen thoroughly in this part of their work, until they have every detail fastened in their minds in its proper logical order. An old salesman of this company should be able to repeat his formula backwards as well as in the regular order—beginning at the middle and working either backward or forward, at will. He understands the "why" and "what for" of every detail of his article and proposition, and is taught to present them in their logical order. Listening to a talk of one of their best salesmen is a liberal education in demonstration.

The essence of this stage of the demonstration is that it should be given in the spirit of a conversational recital of an interesting story, or description of an event. Speak in an impersonal way; that is, avoid suggesting to the prospect that you are trying to sell him the thing. Let this part of your talk be given from the sheer enthusiasm inspired in your mind by the merits of your proposition. Let it be a labor of love—forget all about your hope of sale or profit. Your one aim and object of life, at that moment, should be that of inspiring the prospect with the wonderful merits of your proposition, which you yourself entertain. Yours should be the spirit of the propogandist seeking converts—imparting information for the good of others, and "for the cause." Forget the forthcoming collection plate, in the earnestness of your sermon.

The National Cash Register Company instructs its salesmen as follows regarding this stage of the demonstration: "When you have gotten a prospect to a demonstration you have accomplished a most important step. You can take it for granted that he is to some extent interested in the subject. Now, by all means make the most of that opportunity. Say what you have to say to him thoroughly and carefully. Don't rattle off your demonstration in a hurry, as if you were wound up and had to say so many words to the minute. Give him a chance to speak, to ask questions or make objections. He probably has certain ideas in his mind which may be a decided help or a decided hindrance to your argument. You ought to learn what they are. Don't imagine because he listens in silence that he agrees with you, or even understands all you say. Speak deliberately. If you see from a puzzled or doubtful look on his face that anything is not quite plain to him, stop and make it plain. Take time enough to explain each point thoroughly. Whenever you make a statement that is open to question, be sure to get his assent to it before you proceed. If he will not assent to it exactly as you make it, modify it until he does. Get him to assent in some degree to every proposition you make, so that when you get to the general result he cannot go back and disagree with you. Don't do this however as if you were trying to corner him, but with a simple desire to reach a reasonable basis of argument. Cast aside all attempts at being a clever talker, all idea that there is any trick of words or manner, any secret artfulness about selling registers, and put yourself in the plain, *unaffected spirit of a man who has simply a truth to tell, and is bent upon telling it in the plainest, homliest way. Avoid above all things the fatal mistake of demonstrating to your prospect with a sense of fear, haste, and uncertainty. Realize fully the power of the facts behind you, and have the full confidence of your convictions; coolly and deliberately make each point clear and conclusive, and lead the prospect by simple steps up to absolute conviction."*

If you have held your prospect's interested attention during this stage of the Demonstration, you will find that his imagination is beginning to work in the direction of making mental pictures of how the thing or proposition would work for him—how the article would look in his possession. It is a psychological law that interested investigation, or consideration, tends to awaken the interest of imagination and desire if the object of the investigation blends with the general trend of the person's thought and feelings. The very process of investigation inevitably brings to light new points of interest. And, then, the act of investigation and discovery, instinctively creates a feeling of proprietorship in the thing investigated or discovered. It establishes an association between the object and its investigator.

Halleck says: "* * * We must not forget that any one not shallow and fickle can soon discover something interesting in most objects * * * the attention which they are able to give generally ends in finding a pearl in the most uninteresting looking oyster. * * * The essence of genius is to present an old thing in new ways." And again: "When we think about a thing, or keep the mind full of a subject, the activity in certain brain tracts is probably much increased. As a result of this unconscious preparation, a full fledged image may suddenly arise in consciousness." Hoffding says: "The inter-weaving of the elements of the picture in the imagination takes place in great measure below the threshold of consciousness, so that the image suddenly emerges in consciousness complete in its broad outlines, the conscious result of an unconscious process." Halleck also says: "A representative image of the thing desired is the necessary antecedent to desire. Not until a representative idea comes to the mind does desire arise. It has often been said that where there is no knowledge there can be no desire. A child sees a new toy and wants it. A man notices some improvements about his neighbor's house and wishes them. One nation finds out that another has a war ship of a superior model, and straightway desires something as good or better. A scholar sees a new cyclopedia or work of reference, and desire for it arises. A person returns and tells his friends how delightful a foreign trip is. Their desires for travel increase. Knowledge gives birth to desire, and desire points out the point to will." In this paragraph we have quoted eminent authorities, showing the direct line of psychological progress from interested investigation, through imagination, to desire and will. One investigates and gains favorable knowledge regarding a subject; then his imagination operates to show him the possibility of its successful application to his personal case; then his desire for the thing is awakened.

The stage of Imagination is reached when the prospect begins to think of the thing or proposition in connection with himself. He then begins to picture it in its application to his needs or requirements, or in relation to his general desires, tastes and feelings. The Salesman, in order to awaken the Imagination of the prospect, should endeavor to paint "word pictures" of the thing in its workings, application, value, and utility. He should endeavor to make the prospect see, mentally, the desirability of the thing to any man—how it will work for good; how it will benefit one; how great an advantage it will be for one; how much good it will be in every way for its possessor. Avoid the personal application, even at this late stage—make the application general, so as to avoid scaring off the prospect's pocket book. The whole idea and aim of this stage of the process of sale is to awaken inclination in the prospect—to make his mouth water for the thing—to make him begin to feel that he would like to have it, himself. He must be put into the mental condition of the woman gazing longingly at the hat in the milliner's window; or of the boy who is peeking through the knot-hole in the fence of the base-ball park. He must be led into the feeling that he is on the outside of the fence or window—and the good thing is inside. He will then begin to feel the inclination or desire to "get on the inside."

We once heard a tale of two Southern darkies, which illustrates this point. The two were riding on the same mule's back coming home from work. The foremost darkey began relating the story of some roast possum he had feasted upon the preceding night. He pictured the possum as fat and tender; how they first "briled" him, and then roasted him in the oven; how juicy and brown he looked; how nice he smelt; how he was served up "wid coon-gravy poured all over him;" and finally how nice he tasted when the narrator dug his teeth into him. The darkey in the rear displayed increasing signs of uneasiness as the tale proceeded and as he imagined first the sight, then the smell, and then the taste of the possum. Finally he groaned, and shouted out: "Shet up, yer fool nigger! Does yer wanter make me fall clean offen dis yer mewel?" This is the point—you must make your prospect see, smell and taste the good possum you have, until he is ready to "fall offen de mewel."

Words describing action, taste, feelings, or in fact anything which relates to sense perceptions, tend to arouse the imagination. If the Salesman cultivates the art of actually seeing, tasting or feeling the thing in his own imagination, as he talks, he will tend to re-produce his mental pictures in the mind of his prospect. Imagination is contagious—along the lines of suggestion. Descriptions of sensations, or feelings, tend to awaken a sympathetic response and representation in the minds of others, along the lines of suggestion. Did you never have your imagination and desire fired by the description of a thing—didn't you want to see, feel, or taste it yourself? Did you never feel the effect of words like: "delicious; fragrant; luscious; sweet; mild; invigorating; bracing," etc., in an advertisement? How many young people have been hurried into matrimony by an illustration or word-picture of a "happy home;" "a little wife to meet you at the door;" "little children clustering around you," and all the rest of it? A well known instalment furniture dealer of Chicago is said to be psychologically responsible for thousands of weddings, by his suggestive pictures of the "happy home" and his kind statement that "We will Feather your Nest;" and "You find the Bride, and we will do the rest." The Salesman who can "paint bright pictures in the mind" of his prospect, will succeed in awakening the Imagination, and arousing the Inclination and Desire. Newman well said: "Deductions have no power of persuasion. The heart is commonly reached, not through the reason, but through the imagination. * * * Persons influence us, voices melt us, looks subdue us, deeds inflame us."

And so we pass to the stage of Inclination or Desire, by the road of the Imagination.

The mental state of Inclination, or Desire, following upon the arousing of the appropriate faculties through the Imagination which arises in the stage of Consideration, may be briefly described as the feeling of: "This seems to be a good thing—I would like to have it." This Inclination has been aroused by demonstration and suggestion, and the prospect begins to experience the feeling that the possession of the thing will add to his pleasure, comfort, well-being, satisfaction or profit. You will remember the statement regarding Desire given in a previous chapter: "Desire has for its object something which will bring pleasure or get rid of pain, immediate or remote, for the individual or for some one in whom he is interested. Aversion, or a striving to get away from something, is merely the negative aspect of desire." It is this feeling that you have aroused in some degree in the mind of the prospect. You have brought him to the first stages of Inclination, which naturally brings him to a deliberation as to whether he is justified in purchasing it, and to the point where he will begin to weigh the advantages and disadvantages of the purchase—the question of whether he is willing to "pay the price" for it, which is, after all, the vital question in nearly all forms of deliberation following Inclination and Desire. But as the prospect's mind passes to the stage of Deliberation, you must not lose sight of the question of Desire, for it may be necessary to re-kindle it in him, or to blow upon its sparks, when he debates the "to buy or not to buy." The Deliberation is largely a question of a conflict of motives, and Desire is a powerful motive—so you must be ready to arouse a new phase of "want to" in the prospect to counterbalance some other motive which may be turning the scales in the other direction.

In entering into the stage of Deliberation, or Argument, the discussion passes from the impersonal plane to the personal. The question no longer is: "Is not this a good thing?" to that of "Should you not have it for your own?" This is a distinct change of base, and a different set of faculties are now employed by the Salesman. He leaves the Descriptive phase and enters into that of Argument. He enters into that second meaning or phase of Demonstration which has been defined as: "Proving clearly." And the question of proof and argument is that of whether the prospect is not justified in acquiring the thing. The prospect's mind is already considering the two sides of the question, his Caution combating his Inclination. He is like "Jeppe" of whom we told you in a previous chapter. It is now a question of "my back or my stomach," with him. The Salesman's business now is to demonstrate to him that he can and should acquire the thing. This is a proceeding in which the Salesman's tact, resources, knowledge of human nature, persuasive power, and his logic are needed.

The Salesman has an advantage here which he often overlooks. We refer to the fact that the very objections of the prospect, and his questions give a key to his mental operations, which may be followed up by the Salesman. He knows now what is on the prospect's mind, and what are his general feelings, views, and inclinations regarding the matter. When he begins to talk he gives you a glimpse at his motives, prejudices, hopes and fears. It is quite an art to lead the prospect to ask the questions or to make the objections to which you have a strong answering argument. You then are able to turn back upon him his own argument. It is a psychological fact that the force of a statement made in answer to an interrogative objection, is much stronger than would be the same statement made without the question or objection.

Macbain says: "Lincoln, it is related, early learned in beginning the study of law, that he did not know what it was to prove a thing. By means of careful, conscientious study, in which he took up the problems of Euclid, one by one, he satisfied himself that he then realized absolutely what it meant to prove a proposition. One of the most eminent judges of the Iowa judiciary regards every legal problem as a proposition to be proved by a chain of reasoning. The salesman who determines with absolute accuracy what it means, first, to prove a proposition, and second to apply the general principles of demonstration to an immediate matter in hand, knows just how far to go in making his demonstration, what to include and what to exclude. He can see in his mind's eye the chain of evidence that he is fashioning and will make that fabric of his mind exact, logical and convincing."

(Note:—In order to train the student in logical thinking, development of the logical faculties, and the art of expressing one's thoughts in a logical and effective manner, we would suggest that he make inquiry regarding the volumes of the present series known as "The Art of Logical Thinking, or The Laws of Reasoning;" "Thought-Culture, or Practical Mental Training;" and "The Art of Expression." These books are published by the house issuing the present volume.)

It will be seen that the field of discussion in this stage of Deliberation covers not only the subject of the value and utility of the goods or proposition, but also the question of the price, the advisibility of the purchase at this time, the special advantages possessed, the over-balancing of assumed disadvantages, and in fact the whole question of purchase from beginning to end. The one thing to be held in the mind of the Salesman, however, is "This will do you good; this will do you good; this will do you good!" Keep hammering away at this one nail, in a hundred ways—hold it up to view from a hundred viewpoints and angles. It is the gist of the whole argument, at the last. Don't allow yourself to be sidetracked from this essential proposition, even if the argument spreads itself over a wide field. The point is that (1) the thing is good; (2) the prospect needs it; and (3) that you do him a good turn by making him see that he needs it. We once knew of a very successful life-insurance salesman who had but two points to his selling talk. These were: (1) "Life insurance is a necessity;" and (2) "My company is sound." He brushed aside all other points as immaterial, and insisted with all his heart and soul upon his two points. He was not an educated man, nor was he versed in the technicalities of life-insurance, but he knew his two points from cellar to garret. He outsold many men with actuarial minds, and extended knowledge. He followed the "rifle-ball" policy, instead of the "shot gun" plan. When he struck the target, he made a mark!

It is the Mental Attitude of the Salesman which is the power behind his argumentive rifle-balls. It is his enthusiasm which warms up the prospect's imagination and desire. And, back of these, must always be his belief in his own proposition. The Salesman must "sell himself" over and over again, as friend Holman has suggested. He must answer every objection which occurs to himself, as well as those which are thrust upon him in his work. If the goods are right, there must be an answer to every objection, just as there is a return-move to every move in chess—just as there always is "the other side" to everything. He must find this move, and this "other side" to every objection to which his proposition is open. And he must "sell himself" over and over again, as we have said. The National Cash Register people say to their salesmen: "Selling registers is a straight-forward serious work. You have a plain statement to make of the facts which you are convinced are true, and which you are certain it is for the prospect's benefit to know. You should be as sincere about it as if you were a clergyman preaching the gospel. If you go at it in this sincere spirit the prospect will feel the importance of what you say, and it will carry its due weight. It is a fact which you must fully believe, that the register is a great benefit to any man who buys it; that it will save any merchant many times its cost while he is paying for it."

Pierce says: "So in selling—it is absolutely essential to be genuine. First, last and foremost—be genuine. Practice absolutely what you *preach. Be honest. Never undertake a line of goods that you cannot enthusiastically endorse. Otherwise you cannot 'sell yourself.' And selling one's self is by all means necessary. Students have asked us: 'How about being honest when the customer asks you a question that you know in your heart you cannot answer straight-forwardly?' The answer is: Drop that line; the sooner the better."*

It is true that there are men who "wear the livery of heaven in which to serve the devil," and who practice self-hypnotization upon themselves until they get to actually believe that they are advocating an honest proposition in place of the "fake" they are proposing. And many of these "confidence-men" and "green-goods men" throw themselves so earnestly into their acting that they persuade their victims by reason of their earnestness. We remember Bulwer's tale of the French beggar whose tears wrought havoc upon the hearts of his susceptible victims. "How are you able to weep at will?" he was asked. "I think of my poor father who is dead," he answered. Bulwer adds: "The union of sentiment with the ability of swindling made that Frenchman a most fascinating creature!" But every genuine thing must have its counterfeit—the existence of the latter only serves to prove the former. The success of the "J. Rufus Wallingford's" of real life, are more than equaled by their final downfall. No man can continue to prostitute his talents and be happy, or even ultimately successful. The Law of Compensation is in full operation. No, we're not preaching—just indulging in a little philosophy, that's all!

Let us now proceed to the stage of the Salesman's Closing, and the prospect's Decision and Action.

I love how he talks about the demonstration as a game of checkers or chess. He also points out that prospects *tend to say the same things under the same circumstances, and there is always an appropriate answer.* Entrepreneurs and sales people need to know what their potential customer's objections will be when they are looking to buy or not to buy their product or service.

It's worth spending time looking at the most common objections your prospects will have so you can be prepared to answer every objection they may tell you before you ever pick up the phone to call them. When you know what your prospects concerns are and know how to address them in a confident way, you will close more deals.

He refers to the President of the National Cash Register Company instructing his salespeople to say *"Why, that's the very reason why you should,"* in answering an objection. I recently saw this taught in a webinar. After hearing an objection, the recommended response is "That's the best part! And the very reason you should do this." I'm not sure if the webinar host ever read this book or knew he was using a tactic that was 100 years old. It worked then and it works now.

Another point well taken in this chapter is for the salesperson to keep the presentation moving to the close. Knowing where you are taking the conversation, to the close, will help you address questions effectively and get back on track to making the sale. Prospects come in all shapes and sizes. Credit cards usually come in one. The goal is to help someone get something that is going to help them. You want them to pay you for what you have to help them. Make sure what you have is the right thing for what they need.

A popular sales expert talks about Agree Agree Agree. Always agree with your prospect. Here Atkinson says to *avoid disputes on non-essentials, generalities, and immaterial points. You are not striving for first prize in debate—you're after orders.* These strategies have been in use for generations and the most effective ones have been passed down from top salespeople to top salespeople. It's great to see one foundation these principles were built on today.

He also talks about using stories when you're in the demonstration with a prospect. A very successful SaaS company CEO uses storytelling to make sales. His company grew to 100,000,000 in sales in 3 yrs. He's a great story teller. Stories are an effective way to connect with your prospect. Stories about other client's success can close the deal. Use them.

I'm not sure if you noticed when he was talking about how the prospect starts to imagine how it will be for them to have what is being sold to them. It's really important for people to see how happy they will be when they get whatever it is that you're selling. Whether it's a sense of relief for a problem or a sense of joy to do something they've been wanting to do, they have to embrace your product or service as part of their life in order to buy it. Without that connection for them, the deal won't close.

This quote, *Knowledge gives birth to desire, and desire points out the point to will,* is so vital for a business to succeed. People have to know about you to want to do business with you. If no one knows you and they don't know what you do, how are they going to become your customer? They won't. You have to inform your customers and stay in front of them. You have to be repetitive, consistent, and awesome in how you show up in your customers' lives.

This next reminder is the most important thing a salesperson must do before they attempt to sell anything... *The Salesman must "sell himself" over and over again, as friend Holman has suggested. He must answer every objection which occurs to himself, as well as those which are thrust upon him in his work.*

Pierce says: "So in selling—it is absolutely essential to be genuine. First, last and foremost—be genuine. Practice absolutely what you preach. Be honest. Never undertake a line of goods that you cannot enthusiastically endorse. Otherwise you cannot 'sell yourself.' This has been essential for me in sales. The more sincere and honest I am with people, the more I sell. I've had to leave jobs when I found out that what I was being told to sell wasn't true or what the customer was getting. When I'm not sold, I won't sell even when I try to sell.

CHAPTER FOURTEEN

Secret 12
The Closing
- William Walker Atkinson

The "Closing" is a stage of the sale that is an object of dread to the majority of salesmen. In fact some salesmen content themselves with leading the prospect to the point bordering on Decision and Action, and then lose heart, leave the prospect, and later bring around the sales manager or special "closer" for the concern. They can lead the horse to the trough, but they cannot make him drink. While it is true that the stage of Closing is a delicate one, and involving as it does some practical psychological strategy, nevertheless we are of the opinion that many salesmen are victims of their own adverse auto-suggestions in this matter—they make a boogaboo of the thing which is often found to be but lath and plaster instead of solid iron and granite. Many a salesman is defeated in his Closing by his own fears rather than by the prospect. This stage of the sale is one in which the Salesman should draw on his reserve store of enthusiasm and energy—for he needs it in order to carry the day. As Holman once wrote: "General Grant said that in almost every battle, after hours of fighting, there came a critical moment in which both parties were tired out, and the side that braced up at that moment and pounded hard would win. This is probably so in selling. A good salesman knows that critical moment, and pounds."

The main cause of the failure to bring the prospect to a favorable Decision—the first of the two final stages of the Closing—is that the Salesman has not done his best work in the preliminary stages of the Demonstration. He has not demonstrated the proposition properly, or has not awakened the Imagination and Inclination of the prospect to a sufficient extent. Many salesmen slight the preliminary process of the Demonstration in their anxiety to reach the Closing—but this is a great mistake, for no structure is stronger than its foundation. The Closing should follow as a logical and legitimate conclusion of the preceding stages. It should be like the result of a mathematical problem which has been carefully worked out. Of course it is impossible for any one Salesman to "sell them all," from the very nature of things—but the average man could sell a larger percentage of prospects if he would strengthen himself along the preliminary stages leading up to the Closing, and to the final steps of the latter.

The gist of the whole matter of the failure of a prospect to make a favorable Decision is this: He hasn't been convinced! Why? If you can answer this question, you have the key to the problem. You haven't reached the man's desire. Why? If you can get him to "want" the thing, the decision is a mere matter of final settling down to choice. You may have said to the man, "This is a good thing—you ought to have it," over and over again—but have you actually made him see that it was a good thing and that he ought to have it? It is one thing to tell a man these things, and another to reproduce your own beliefs in his mind.

The changing of the talk from that affecting Deliberation on the part of the prospect, to that influencing his Decision, is a delicate matter. There is a "psychological moment" for the change which some men seem to perceive intuitively, while others have to learn it by hard experience. It is the critical balancing point between "enough" and "too much" talk.

On the one hand, the Salesman must beware of a premature Closing, and on the other he must avoid "unselling" a man after he has made the psychological sale. Some men are inclined toward one of these faults—

and some to the other. The ideal Salesman has found the nice point of balance between the two.

If the Salesman attempts to make a premature Closing, he will probably have failed to bring about the full desire and careful Deliberation in the prospect's mind. As a practical writer on the subject has pointed out, this course is as faulty as that of a lawyer who would attempt to begin his closing address to the jury before he had gotten in his evidence. The trained finger on the pulse should detect the "high-tide of interest," and close the demonstration at this point, moving surely and swiftly to the Closing.

On the other hand, if the Salesman persists in talking on, rambling and wandering, after he has made a particular point, or all of his points, he runs the risk of losing his prospect's attention and interest, and with it the newly awakened inclination and desire. James H. Collins, in a recent article in "The Saturday Evening Post," relates the following amusing anecdote illustrating this tendency on the part of the Salesman:

"How easily a customer may be talked out of buying is shown by the experience of a real-estate promoter who sells New York property to investors in other cities through a staff of salesmen. One of his men reported that he was unable to close an elderly German in Pittsburg. 'I've explained the whole property,' said the salesman. 'He understands the possibilities, yet doesn't invest.' Next time the promoter was in Pittsburg he called on this investor, accompanied by his salesman. The latter explained the proposition again most exhaustively, and made every effort to be clear and convincing. * * * From time to time the investor tried to interrupt, but the salesman swept on, saying: 'Just a moment, and I'll take that point up with you.' When the story was finished he recapitulated. When that was finished he began a resume of the recapitulation preparatory to rushing the man. Here the boss felt that the investor really wanted to be heard, so he interrupted the salesman: 'Charlie, I guess if Mr. Conrad here doesn't realize the magnificent opportunities in New York realty after all you've told him, there's no use telling him any more.' 'Mein gracious!' protested Conrad. 'I do realize them. What I wanted to say is that I will take these lots.'"

There is a sixth sense, or intuitive faculty developed in many good salesmen which tends to inform them when they have said enough along any particular line, or on the whole subject. In the midst of a sentence, or after the close of a statement, one will notice a subtle and indefinable change in the manner or expression of the prospect which informs one that it is time to stop, and "sum up," or briefly recapitulate. And this "summing up" must be made briefly, and to the point, in an earnest manner. It should be made in a logical order and sequence, each point being driven in as with a sledge hammer of conviction. One should lay especial stress upon any points in which the prospect seemed interested during the Demonstration. In short he should fall in with the spirit of the attorney in his closing address, in which he sums up his strong points, always with an eye on the jury which he has carefully watched for signs of interest during the progress of the trial. Each juryman's character is represented by a faculty in the mind of the prospect—each should be appealed to along its own particular lines.

The perception of the "psychological moment" of closing the selling talk, is akin to that of the lawyer who leads his jury up to a dramatic and logical climax—and then stops. Avoid creating an anti-climax. Mr. Collins in the magazine article mentioned a moment ago says: "The chief shortcoming of the salesman who has difficulty in closing is, usually, that he doesn't know when the psychological moment has come to rush his man. This is a very definite moment in every deal. Veteran salesmen gauge it in various ways, some by the attention their argument is receiving, others by some sign in the customer's eyes, and others still by a sort of sixth sense which seldom leads them wrong. * * * If the mechanism of a representative sale could be laid bare for study it would probably approximate the mechanism of the universe in that material theory by which the philosophers explain the whole thing up to the point where a slight push was necessary to set it going eternally. The sale of the man who doesn't close is technically complete except for the push that lands the order. Sales may be made by patient exposition of facts, building up the case for the goods. But to close them, very often, a real push or kick is needed. Logic avails up to the moment when the customer must be rushed."

The trouble with some prospects is that they have practically made the Decision—but do not know they have. That is, they have accepted the premises of the argument; admitted the logic of the succeeding argument and demonstration; can see no escape from the conclusion—but still they have not released the spring of formal Decision which settles the matter with a mental "click." It is the Salesman's business to produce this mental "click." It is a process akin to "calling the hand" of the opponent in a certain game other than that of salesmanship. It is the stage in which the matter is fairly and squarely "put up" to the prospect. It is a situation demanding nerve on the part of the Salesman—that is apparent nerve, for it is after all somewhat of a bluff on his part, for although he wins if the prospect says "Yes," he does not necessarily lose if the answer be "No!" for the Salesman, like the lover, should never let one "No" discourage him. "Never take 'No!' for an answer," says the old song—and it is worth remembering by the Salesman.

The "click" of Decision is often produced by the Salesman "putting up" some strong question or statement to the prospect, which, in the popular term, "brings him to his feet." As for instance the closing illustration of some of the National Cash Register salesmen, who after having demonstrated the merits of the cash register by placing in it the "$7.16 of real money," in two-dollar bills, one-dollar bills, silver dollars, half-dollars, quarters, dimes, nickles and pennies, during the various points of the demonstration, turns suddenly to the prospect and says to him: "Mr. Blank, you have been watching every coin and bill I have put into this cash drawer. Now how much money do you think is in this drawer?" Mr. Blank naturally doesn't know. Then the Salesman proceeds: "Well, then, if you have no conception of the amount of money in this drawer, after watching me put every coin and bill into it, far more closely than you could possibly watch such transactions in your own store, you must admit you are guessing every night as to the amount that should be in your cash drawer in your store." Pausing a moment to let this strong point sink into the prospect's mind, the Salesman then says, earnestly and impressively: "Mr. Blank, don't you think you ought to have a register of this kind?" Every proposition contains features similar to the one noted above, which can be used effectively in bringing about the "click" of decision.

In some cases the Suggestion of Imitation may be employed at this stage by showing orders from others, provided they are of importance. Some men do not like this, but the majority are influenced by the example of others and the imitative suggestion prevails and brings down the scale of Decision. In some other cases the Salesman has found it advantageous to drop into a serious, earnest tone, manifesting a spirit akin to that of the earnest worker at a revival meeting, and laying his hand on the prospect's arm, impress upon him the urgent need of his doing this thing for his own good. With some prospects this plan of placing the hand upon him in a brotherly spirit, and looking him earnestly in the eye, results in the final warming up of conviction and decision—probably from the associated suggestion of previous solemn exhortations and friendly counsel. But other men resent any such familiarity—one must know human nature in using this method.

Never attempt to close your sale in the presence of outsiders. Always defer it until the prospect is alone, and you have his undivided attention. It is impossible to get into the "heart to heart" rapport in the presence of other people.

You may sometimes bring about the Decision by asking pointed and appropriate questions, the answer of which must act to clinch the matter. But in asking these questions always be careful not to ask a question which may easily be answered by a "No." Never say: "Won't you buy?" or "Can't I sell you?" These questions, and others like them give the suggestion of a negative answer—they make it too easy for the prospect to say "No." Remember what we have said elsewhere regarding the suggestions of questions. Remember the horrible example of *"You don't want to buy anything to-day, do you?"* And also remember that a question preceded by an affirmative statement, tends to draw forth an affirmative answer. As, for instance: *"That is a nice day, isn't it;"* or, *"This is a beautiful shade of pink, isn't it?;"* or, *"This is quite an improvement, isn't it?"* In asking the important question, do not show any doubt in your tone, manner or form of expression. Beware, always, of making a negative mental track for your prospect to travel over. The mind works along the lines of least resistance—be sure you make that *"line"* in the right direction.

In cases where you have been recommended to call upon a person by a friend with whom he has discussed the proposition, you may often find that but little preliminary talk is needed, and you may proceed to the Closing very shortly after opening the conversation. In these cases, the prospect often has *"closed himself"* without your aid—he wants the thing without urging. When you meet this condition, take things for granted, and make the sale just as you would if the prospect had called upon you to make the purchase. And in any and every case, if you see that the prospect has *"closed himself,"* clinch the matter at once. And you can readily see when this stage has arrived. After all, the process of discovering the *"psychological moment"* of Closing is like the intuitive discovery of the psychological moment for *"popping the question"* in courting. At certain times in courting these psychological moments arise—then is the time to *"close."* And the same rule holds good in Salesmanship. It is largely a matter of feeling, after all.

And, in Salesmanship, as in courting, remember also that *"Faint Heart never won Fair Lady."* Fortune favors the brave. When you feel the psychological urge of the moment—step in! Don't be afraid. Remember the old couplet:

"Tender-handed grasp a nettle, and it stings you for your pains.

Grasp it like a man of mettle, and it soft as down remains."

When it comes to the psychological moment, banish fear from your mind. Show spirit and be *"game."* You have got to make the plunge, and take the risk of *"the proposal"* some time—why not now? You have done *your best, then go ahead. Stand up and take your chance like a man. But never act as if there is any chance about it—preserve your mental attitude of confident expectation, for these mental states are contagious.*

If, in spite of everything, the Decision be against you, do not be discouraged. If you think you can reverse the decision by a little further persuasion, do so by all means. Many a battle is won, after it has apparently been lost. Few maidens expect their gallant laddies to accept the first "No" as conclusive — and the minds of many buyers work in the same way. There is a certain coyness about maids, and prospects, which seems to call for a little further coaxing. Many prospects yield only at the final appeal—they are like Byron's heroine who "saying she would ne'er consent, consented."

But if the "No" is final, take it good-naturedly, and without show of resentment, and assuming an "I will call again another day" spirit, bid the prospect good-bye, courteously, and take your departure. Many subsequent sales have been made in this way—and many have been lost by a show of ill-nature. The average man likes a game fighter, and respects a "good loser." Don't give up at anything short of a "knockout," but, that given, shake hands with the victor good-naturedly, and then proceed to lay plans for another interview. Good nature and cheerfulness under defeat never fail to make friends, and to disarm enemies.

As we have said in a previous chapter, there is sometimes a hitch between Decision and Action. The spirit of procrastination creeps in, and the prospect tries to put off the actual order. Try to overcome this by "taking down" the order at once. Do not allow any wait at this stage. If no signed order is necessary get the order down in your order book as quickly as possible. Have your order book handy so that no awkward wait arises. Avoid these intervals of waiting as far as possible. Get through with the thing, and get out.

If a signed order is required, approach the request as a matter of course. Do not assume the air of asking any further favor, or of needing any argument regarding the signing. Treat it as a matter of course, and as if the matter had been agreed upon. Do not say "I will have to ask you to sign," etc., but say simply "sign here, please," placing your fountain pen at the "suggestive slant," and in his direction, indicating the line at the same time. Some salesmen even touch the pen to the line, starting the ink flowing and the suggestion operating with the one movement. Others proceed, calmly, like this: "Let's see, Mr. Blank, what is your shipping address (or street number)?" adding, "We can have these goods here by about such-and-such a date." And while he is saying this they are filling up the order blank. Then, in the most matter of fact, business-like manner they lay the order before the prospect, indicating the line for signature, and saying: "Now, if you will kindly sign here, please, Mr. Blank." And it is all over.

Always have the order blank, or book, and the fountain pen handy. Avoid fiddling around after the pen or the book, or both—this is suggestive in the wrong direction. Some salesmen lay the pen on top of the order book, and place them easily before the prospect while talking. Others lay the pen by the side of the book, in the same way. Collins says: "One of the leading newspapers in the Middle West has a school for the canvassers who solicit subscriptions. A set of books is sold in connection with a year's subscription to this paper, and the solicitors are drilled in old fashioned bookselling tactics, learning their argument by rote. At the precise point where the signature of the prospect is to be secured the salesman is taught to take his pencil from his pocket, drop it on the floor apparently by accident, stoop over and pick it up as he finishes his argument, and put it into the prospect's fingers as a matter of course. Six times in ten the signature is written without more argument." The psychological point employed here is evidently that of distracting the prospect's mind from his ordinary objection, and attracting his attention to the recovered pencil. A similar proceeding is that followed by certain salesmen who carry a large fountain pen with a rubber band wrapped around the handle. Talking cheerfully, they drop the pen on the prospect's desk, close to his hand. The rubber band makes it fall noiselessly, and prevents it from rolling. The prospect is *said usually to involuntarily pick up the pen, and move it toward the order book which has been deftly placed before him, and, then, still absorbed in the talk of the Salesman, he signs the order blank. These methods are given for what they are worth, and in the way of illustrating a psychological principle. Personally, we do not favor these methods, and prefer the orthodox fountain pen, courteously handed the prospect, at the "suggestive slant," with possibly the point touching the line as an illustration of the "on this line, please," which accompanies it.*

The principle to be observed in all cases where orders have to be signed, receipts made out, etc., is to make the process as easy as possible for the prospect. Let him work along the line of the least resistance. Avoid giving him the adverse suggestion of "red tape," formality, "iron-clad contracts," etc. Act upon the principle of the young man who when he asked his father for money would say it very smoothly and rapidly "twenty dollars please," as if it were twenty cents. Smooth away every item of delay and friction, and adopt the "rubber tire and ball bearings" mental attitude and mode of procedure.

Regarding the much disputed and vexing question of the interval between Decision and Action, and the frequent failure of Decision to take form in Action—which question, by the way, is very important in the Closing of the Salesman—we ask you to read the following from the pen of Prof. William James, the eminent psychologist:

"We know what it is to get out of bed on a freezing morning in a room without a fire, and how the very vital principle within us protests against the ordeal. Probably most persons have lain on certain mornings for an hour at a time unable to brace themselves to the resolve. We think how late we shall be, how the duties of the day will suffer; we say, 'I must get up, this is ignominious,' etc.; but still the warm couch feels too delicious, the cold outside too cruel, and resolution faints away and postpones itself again and again just as it seemed on the verge of bursting the resistance and passing over into the decisive act. Now how do we ever get up under such circumstances? If I may generalize from my own experience, we more often than not get

up *without any struggle or decision at all. We suddenly find that we have to get up. A fortunate lapse of consciousness occurs; we forget both the warmth and the cold; we fall into some reverie connected with the day's life, in the course of which the idea flashes across us, 'Hello! I must lie here no longer'—an idea which at that lucky instant awakens no contradictory or paralyzing suggestions, and consequently produces immediately its appropriate motor effects. It was our acute consciousness of both the warmth and cold during the period of struggle, which paralyzed our activity then and kept our idea of rising in the condition of wish and not of will. The moment these inhibitory ideas ceased, the original idea exerted its effects. This case seems to me to contain in miniature form the data for an entire psychology of volition."*

Prof. James, in another place, gives the following additional hint of the process of transmuting the Decision into Action: *"Let us call the last idea which in the mind precedes the motor discharge, 'the motor-cue' * * * There can be no doubt whatever that the cue may be an image either of the resident or the remote kind."*

It will be seen then that the "motor cue" which releases the spring of Action—the mental trigger which fires the gun of will—may easily be some remote idea suggested to the mind, as for instance the sight of the slanted fountain pen and order book. The man wants to, but does not feel like getting out of bed, and his mind becomes inactive on the question. If some friend had said to him, "Come, get out old fellow;" or if he had had his mind suddenly attracted by some outside sound or sight, he would have sprung out at once. As we have said, elsewhere, the placing of a piece of twisted paper in the ear of a horse will cause him to forget his balkiness—it changes his current of thought. Any new impulse will tend to get a man over his period of "I want to but I don't" mental hesitancy. We may have given you the psychology of the thing here—you must work it out in the details of application to suit your own requirements. Learn to show your prospect something that will cause him to spring out of bed. Learn to stick the piece of twisted paper in his ear, to overcome his balkiness. Give him the "motor cue" by supplying him with a mental image "either of the resident or remote kind." Like the boy shivering on the brink of the stream, he needs but a "little shove" to make him take the plunge. Then he will call to others: "Come on in, the water's fine."

And, now in conclusion: You have the signed order, but you must continue your Mental Attitude until you fade from the prospect's sight. Do not gush or become maudlin, as we have seen salesmen do. Maintain your balance, and thank your customer courteously, but not as the recipient of alms. Keep up his good impression of and respect for you to the last. Leave the prospect with this thought radiating from your mind: "I have done this man a good turn." The prospect will catch these subtle vibrations, in some way not worth discussing, and he too will feel that he has done well. Avoid the "Well, I landed this chap, all right, all right!" mental attitude, which shows so plainly in the manner of some salesmen after they have booked an order. The prospect will catch those vibrations also, and will not like it—he will resent it, naturally. In short, you would do well to follow the homely but scientific advice of the old salesman who said: "Keep your sugar-coating on to the last—leave 'em with a pleasant taste in their mouths." Make a good Last Impression as well as a good First Impression.

But—and remember this also—get away when your work is over. Do not hang around the office or store of the prospect after the sale is made. Do not place yourself in a position where some newly discovered objection will cause you to do your work all over again. You have got what you came for—now get out! As Macbain says: "When the close is made the customer should be left in the shortest possible time that may not be characterized as abrupt. Having 'talked a man into a sale,' the salesman should be careful not to talk him out. The old adage, 'Stop praising the goods after the sale is made,' is as true as it is trite." Collins very aptly says on this point: "The explainer type of salesman may actually sell goods to a customer and then, by staying and talking, unsell him without knowing it. * * * One afternoon not long ago, for instance, a salesman sold eleven thousand dollars' worth of fabrics to a prominent merchant and, by staying for a friendly chat after the order had been secured, gave the merchant time to think twice and cancel it. An excellent rule is that of a salesman who built up a business to a quarter million in competition with wealthy competitors, doing this by sheer selling ability. 'Take the first train out of town after you sell your man,' was his rule. If there was no train for several hours he excused himself the moment a deal was closed, and disappeared. 'Just as sure as I stayed around after that order was in my pocket,' he says, 'part of it would be cancelled or modified by the buyer, or some of my work in selling undone. If it were nothing else the buyer would play on the fact that I felt good about getting that order, and squeeze something extra out of me.' When you land your man get out of sight."

And, taking our own advice, kind reader, we, having said our say and "closed," will now take our departure. We thank you for your kind attention, and feel that we "have done you a good turn."

It's interesting to note that salespeople have been afraid to close for over 100 years. When I was training sales reps, many of them were lost on what to say to get a prospect to sign up for the service and would just say they would call the prospect back so they could think about it. They didn't last long in their sales job.

Atkinson points out that the salesperson's ability to close depends largely on how well they did the previous steps to get there. There is a process to selling. And using that process will bring success. Most every profession has a success process that when implemented leads to consistent positive results. For sales, it's best to establish your selling process for your business and follow it.

The analogy of an attorney making their closing arguments makes a lot of sense when it comes to closing. If the prospect hasn't been given all the evidence and doesn't fully imagine how this product or service is going to benefit them, the prospect won't be convinced in their own mind to buy. This is why having a sales process to follow will help you close more deals. You'll be taking the prospect through a series of steps to help them make their decision to buy.

The finesse of the close is a bit of an art. Having closing questions and closing statements prepared in advance so you know what you are going to say is very helpful. One I like to use after a prospect has been asking questions is, "Do you have any other questions before you sign up?" Create a lot of different questions and answers so you have different things to say. There are hundreds of closes you can come up with. Do it.

When he talks about thinking well of the person who just bought from you and how you did right by him reminds me of a shop owner in Telluride, CO I knew. I lived there for 4 ½ years.. She had a rule in her store with her employees. They were not allowed to say anything negative about any customer that had walked into the store. She believed in a subtle way, the customer would pick up on their negative thoughts about them and they wouldn't come back.

In sales, I believe from my experience, that it's important to decide to like the people you are talking to. When I coached sales reps that were doing a lot of cold calling, I would tell them they needed to like people when they called, even if they didn't answer the phone or weren't that nice to them when they called. Not everyone is going to be easy to connect with. Deciding to like them first will make it easier.

Every call, every voicemail, every email has to be done with the right attitude. People want to be liked, people want to be cared about, people want help when they need something they can't get or do by themselves. Sales people can do a lot for other people when they are genuinely nice and care about their prospects.

And his ending is a great close. When the sales is completed don't linger.

CHAPTER FIFTEEN

Conclusion

When I was putting this book together, I wanted to find sales wisdom of the ages. Seeing how some things haven't changed...people are people and we operate how people have always operated...was really interesting to me. Being able to source back through generations to find sales techniques being taught today gave me a new context and appreciation for the sales craft.

My hope is that, while the 12 Secrets I've presented incorporated more than 12 things, my goal of presenting 2 vantage points to the sales person's ultimate success will give you a better grasp of what might be missing in your approach to sales. PT Barnum and William Walker Atkinson had some overlap in what they covered. The wisdom they shared with their readers is still as relevant today as it was back then.

The bottom line is, there is an overall picture you need to have about yourself with your success. You have to have a compelling reason that keeps you in the game. You have to keep learning, keep trying, and keep finding ways to improve what you do. You need to figure out what you can sell someone by understanding what you can do for them that they need.

If you're interested in learning more, feel free to contact me at laura@416sales.com.

416 Sales - The Ultimate Success Planner

Available on Amazon

Your Ultimate Tool For Your Ultimate Success!

 Kathy

★★★★★ **This is a great way to organize your business goals.**
September 9, 2019
Format: Paperback

I'm a big believer in setting goals. I'm a big believer in becoming hyper focused on a few tasks that must be completed. This planner helps you keep your goals and focus in one spot. I've followed the Dan Sullivan strategy of mapping out my next 90 days for many years now, but they are on loose leaf papers. Sometimes I lose them for good and other times to the pile of 'to do's' on my desk. By having it all in one book, I will be able to retain my focus even better. I also love that it's not based on a year. You start where you are today and go through the end of the book. No more throwing planners away.

Set your goals and track your progress with quarterly, monthly, and weekly pages. 416 Sales - The Ultimate Success Planner was designed to give you a blueprint for your own success and help keep you accountable with your goals throughout the year. Having the 416 Sales - The Ultimate Success Planner will give you the space you need to write out your success game plan to achieve your ultimate dreams. Carry this planner with you and use it for notes and observations in addition to planning and creating your ideal life. Get yours today!

I wish you the best success in everything you do!

Laura Burton